Coping with Germany

To the memory of Reggie

# Coping with Germany

John A. S. Phillips

Cartoons by David Austin

Basil Blackwell

Copyright © John A. S. Phillips 1989

First published 1989

Basil Blackwell Ltd
108 Cowley Road, Oxford, OX4 1JF, UK

Basil Blackwell Inc.
432 Park Avenue South, Suite 1503
New York, NY 10016, USA

*British Library Cataloguing in Publication Data*

Phillips, John A. S.
  Coping with Germany.
  1. Germany – Visitors' guides
  I. Title
  914.3'04878
ISBN 0–631–16048–5
ISBN 0–631–16049–3 Pbk

*Library of Congress Cataloging in Publication Data*

Phillips, John A. S.
  Coping with Germany/John A.S. Phillips.
    p.   cm.

  Includes index.
  ISBN 0–631–16048–5     ISBN 0–631–16049–3 (pbk.)
    1. Germany—Description and travel—1945– —Guide-books.
I. Title.
DD16.P55 1989
914.3'04878—dc19

Typeset in 10 on 11½ pt Garamond
by Opus, Oxford
Printed in Great Britain by Billing & Sons Ltd, Worcester

# Contents

# Preface

Having lived on and off in Germany since 1964, for the last 16 years more on than off, I no longer see Germany with English eyes but with eyes that have become partly German – although I still become confused in post offices, despite probably knowing perforce more about German postal regulations than many Germans. I do not see Germany as a tourist or visitor any more, but what I see I have mulled over many times and also discussed with other foreign visitors to the country. Sometimes I have borrowed my friends' eyes, their experiences and reactions. The responsibility of sifting through and interpreting these various experiences is of course mine.

I might not always have been successful. Some personal prejudice or simple misunderstanding might have obscured things, caused me to generalize from a personal experience. Often it is very difficult to do anything else. That is why I would welcome criticism, discussion and suggestions for improvement from others.

# Acknowledgements

So many people have helped me, and it is embarrassing not always to have been able to note down their names or, having done so, find the piece of paper on which I scribbled my helper's name. I might well, in any case, have misunderstood it over the phone. The following are the kind people whose names I did record or reconstruct, from memory or by tracking them down again. I feel especially guilty because the anonymous helpers were usually those whom I just managed to get hold of before they went home on a Friday afternoon when I desperately needed a fact or figure, the ignorance of which was driving me crackers. Some officials, in both Germany and England, even answered fiddly questions over the weekend.

The following people allowed me to pester them at some length by letter, telephone or, worse still, in person.

*In Austria:*

Herr Dr Müll, Federal Chancellor's Office.

*In Germany:*

Frau Adler, German National Tourist Board, Frankfurt; Frau Bannasch, Press Officer, Tourist Office, Bielefeld; Herr Ltd. Forstpräsident Edmund Bauer, Bayreuth; Herr Dipl.-Volksw. Univ. Wolfgang Berlinghof, Regierung von Oberfranken; Herr Dr Phil. Albrecht Graf von und zu Egloffstein, MA, Kulturdirektor, Bezirksheimatpfleger von Oberfranken; Frau Hannelore Egold, Pressestelle, Flughafen Frankfurt/M. AG; Herr A. Engerer, Landw. Direktor, Regierung von Oberfranken and his assistant Herr Amtmann Richard Müller; Herr Franke, Pressestelle, Flughafen Frankfurt/M. AG; Robert Fraser, Esq., Munich; Fräulein Christine Freise, Bayreuth University; Herr Abteilungsdirektor Horst Fürbringer, Bayerisch Hypotheken- und Wechsel-Bank, Bayreuth; Herr Postamtmann Dieter Heider, Bayreuth; Herr Dr W. Hennig, Deutsches Institut für Normung e.V., Berlin; Herr Pharmaciedirektor Howarth, Regierung von Oberfranken; Herr Hans-Joachim König, Bayreuth University; Herr Professor Dr Kurt Kluxen, Erlangen; Herr Oscar Maisel and Herr Peter Rützenhöfer, Gebrüder Maisel's Bierbrauerei, Bayreuth; Herr Olesch, Federal Post Office; S.E. Alram Graf von und zu Ortenburg, Tambach; Fräulein Sibylle Peters, Bayreuth University; Herr N. Rosenthal, Fleischer GmbH; Herr Alexander Ross, Bayreuth University; Herr Adolf Schindlbeck, Bahnhofsrestaurant, Bayreuth; David Taylor, Esq., Munich; Frau Erika Tichay, Gaststätte Herzoghöhe (Laus), Bayreuth; Frau Professor Dr Gertrud Walter, Erlangen; Herr Willy Wild, Spielwaren Wild, Bayreuth; Herr Georg Wimmer, Bayerischer Bauernverband; Herr Postamtmann Siegfried Wolf, Bayreuth;

and the following institutions:

Bayerische Staatsregierung; Staatsministerium für Arbeit und Sozialordnung; Staatsministerium des Innern; Allgemeiner Deutscher Automobil Club e.V., Bayreuth.

*In the German Democratic Republic:*

Frau Müller, Potsdam Tourist Board; Frau Müller, Potsdam Informationen.

*In England:*

Michael Dillon Esq., Director of the Leipzig Air Agency, London; Mrs Sandra Dreelan, M. Sae Director, Camp and Outdoor Leisure Association; Herr W. Martin Dünz, (West) German National Tourist Office, London; Fräulein Rita Samwald, Rycote Park; Herr Kurt Schubert (Director) and Mrs

Sheila Taylor of Berolina Travel Limited, Tourist Office of the German Democratic Republic; Bridgette Sheppy;

and the following organizations:

British Rail; The Automobile Association; Royal Automobile Association.

*In the USA:*

German National Tourist Board in Los Angeles; Colleen McDermott.

Frau Margot Lenich, Bayreuth, typed the manuscript with her usual diligence and dedication.

In conclusion I would like to record my gratitude to my copy editor, Dr Mary Shields, whom I have known for many years and who took immense trouble with the manuscript. My friend and former colleague, Dr Dennis de Loof, has been a tower of strength. I have benefited greatly from his kindness and wisdom. Mrs Max Michaelis's kind hospitality and sagacity at Rycote Park, near Oxford, was of great assistance when submitting the manuscript. Finally, I wish to thank my cousin, the Rt Hon The Lord Joseph of Portsoken in the City of London CH PC, whose hospitality in London and astringent criticism have always been of such help to me in my writings both German and English.

I am, of course, responsible for all the mistakes which, however hard one tries to avoid them, are forever present.

# Introduction

There is a sense in which West Germany is not completely German any more because of its new-found internationalism. It has been strongly influenced by America and Britain following the last war and is being subjected to the influences of Japanese management and competition; it is also by no means indifferent to Australian culture. One has to leave the cities and towns, drive deep into the country and try to shut oneself off from the outside world to experience what one feels must be the real Germany.

But is there a 'real Germany' at all? Can one in the Common Market talk of national entities any more? It all depends on how one experiences a country, whether as traveller or resident. It is the depth of experience which counts and how deep one as a visitor wants to go. Of course, life all round the world is the same for many people at many superficial and some profound levels – for business people, constantly on the move in planes and staying in Sheraton hotels, even for senior citizens travelling by train and eating at McDonald's.

My answer is a simple one: forget the tourist sights, the castles, cathedrals, art galleries and museums; just plunge into everyday life, get on a tram, go into a post office, buy a cup of coffee or a sausage at a stall. Do the things the locals do. Get things wrong. Get hopelessly lost. Ask someone to help you. Meet people. I like sitting in a German pub, eating, reading, writing and just observing people, talking to them and trying to understand the sort of lives they lead.

**About the book**

This is not a guide book, but a companion for those visiting Germany for the first time or for those who come back for more and want to know what goes on behind the scenes of tourist life. It is meant more for the visitor than the tourist, or for the tourist who wants to be a visitor.

It is particularly intended for those business people whose lack of German and lack of knowledge of the country make them hold back on exporting to the Federal Republic. I have been told that many potential exporters are inhibited in this way. I should be thrilled if this book could help these people to conquer their fears. I can assure anyone who feels that German markets are too strange to handle that any initial difficulties can be overcome. A good product sells the world over, and especially in Germany where people are so quality- and value-conscious. It is a friendly country, but the customs *are* different.

**Changing Germany**

One thing I have become very aware of is that Germany has changed since the last war. Carlo Schmid, when Vice President of the *Bundestag* (the German parliament), is quoted as saying after the war that 'German youth needs to be educated to disobedience.' During the sixties his wish was fulfilled with a vengeance as the flame of revolution was ignited at universities. Professors were shouted down in lectures and seminars. Things got out of control. A vocal minority seemed to be taking over. In my opinion, however, although student revolt was undoubtedly significant, it was not the type of German experience which represents what I term the typical German way of life. The same holds for the terrorist groups which sprang up – in the Baader-Meinhof group and the Red Army Faction – and for those who still saw off electric train poles and blow up government buildings.

What I feel to be much more significant, new and a truly German political phenomenon is the emergence of the Greens as a political party which, whether one agrees with its philosophy or not, is determined to preserve our heritage of fresh air, fresh water and the glory of nature. In this movement, I would argue that what Carlo Schmid wanted has occurred. However, this nonconformist Germany is not what I am writing about.

This book is essentially about the Federal Republic, that is, West Germany. There is, however, one chapter devoted exclusively to East Germany, the German Democratic Republic. I would in no way claim to be an expert on the different political system practised there, which in many respects makes it a completely different country.

Recently Herr Erich Honecker, the East German Communist Party Secretary and Head of State, visited the Federal Republic. It was a profoundly moving experience for all. One only hopes that at some stage it leads to the disappearance of the inhuman wall which divides the two countries. It was following his visit to his parents' grave in Saarland that Herr Honecker said for the first time in the Federal Republic that he could envisage a day when the frontier between the two Germanies would be like the unfortified GDR–Polish frontier; and that the East–West German border would no longer express division but unity.

**The Federal Republic of Germany and the German Democratic Republic**

For some potential visitors, war associations die hard, as they do in Germany too. It should be realized that there the guiltless suffered more than the guilty. Hitler, an Austrian, is still an embarrassment to Germans. His memory will never be expunged. Germany is still divided between East and West as a result. East Germans get shot in the back escaping crossing the Iron-Curtained border. The political realities of German life are too stark to forget simply because of the post-war industrial miracle (*Wirtschaftswunder*). The sites of the concentration camps are still there, haunting warnings of past horrors and an uncertain future should dreaded World War III break out. There are tensions beneath the tourist glitter, fairy-tale castles and beer-drinking festivals.

Surely all this makes a visit to capitalist West Germany, not forgetting the East if one wants to experience the 'workers' and peasants' state', all the more interesting and worthwhile. The face of Germany is none the less attractive for being lined. Despite the past, the British or American visitor is assured of a welcome – especially from ex-prisoners

**The legacy of the last war**

of war, should one be lucky enough to meet them. German POW's usually have something nice to say about British gaolers. They recognize a basic British decency but also an old-fashioned eccentricity which intrigues them even more. Go to Germany and you will be helped and hosted, not, as in some other countries, fleeced, though there are strategies recommended in this book which should prevent one being outwitted too outrageously. And there is the added bonus of most Germans – high and low – being able to speak at least some English, often very well. Some visitors will be startled to find that Germans, in general, admire, like and are intrigued by the British, though they have reservations about football hooligans.

**German efficiency**

West Germany represents efficiency, sometimes crude and thrusting, in commerce and industry. It is a society of go-getters. People usually work and play hard (there are exceptions, for example civil servants!). All classes – especially the workers – are prosperous, because they have earned prosperity within the framework of a society and economy which favours enterprise and discourages sloth or failure. There is an excellent health and workers' insurance system amounting to a welfare state, but not of the British 'cradle to to the grave' type (there is no state assistance for strikers' families, for example). Things are organized in such a way that workers may not and do not go on strike. Trains run on time; gas, electricity, water and sewage services are seldom, if ever, interrupted, though Lufthansa (the national airline) on occasion has industrial troubles. Things work, so do people. A visitor can usually rely on promised goods and services being available.

There are of course disadvantages in the pursuit of excellence. Germans, in general, are excellent at doing things – building motorways, sprucing up cities, breaking industrial records with reliable cars and washing machines. Not only are there resultant environmental hazards, but Germans sometimes have difficulty in relaxing. They are differently structured to us. Apart from political activists, social drop-outs and other dissatisfied groups, they tend to be more ambitious. In other words: life is different, not only in superficial, sausage-consuming, beer-drinking ways, but fundamentally in personal communication, in business and personal behaviour. This is nothing to worry about. However, it is with the aim of unravelling such differences that *Coping with Germany* has been written. The aim is to 'cope' by understanding the people, their ways and customs.

Germans tend to think and act in a certain programmed way. Germany as opposed to America, France and England is – apart from its younger generation – less a country of individualists. The whole structure of society, way of life, constitution, legal system, in fact everything, often ensures conformity. Why and how are the questions this book seeks to answer.

Now for a brief description of the country itself. The ten individual *Länder* which constitute the Federal Republic comprise the large metropolises of Hamburg (between Lower Saxony and Schleswig Holstein) and Bremen in the north, and the largest of the *Länder*, the Free State of Bavaria, which borders on the East German and Czechoslovakian as well as the Austrian borders, in the south. In between are the *Länder* of North-Rhine-Westphalia (the industrial centre of the country with the Ruhr) and Hessen (with Germany's commercial centre, Frankfurt), together with Rhineland-Palatinate, Saarland and Baden-Württemberg (with Stuttgart and the Mercedes-Benz factories), which in the west border Switzerland and France.

**Topography**

Berlin lies in East Germany. West Berlin has its own Lord Mayor but, like the Eastern sector of the city, is still under the Allied Control Commission. It thus has a different status from the rest of the Federal Republic. It is reachable by air (along the celebrated corridor), by rail or by motorway, the latter two being subject to control by the East Germans.

As in the United Kingdom, there is much variety within a relatively small area. (The whole of West Germany would fit comfortably into the state of

Minnesota, USA.) The flat plains of the north with their large heaths (e.g. the Lüneburger Heide) and forests yield to low mountain ranges; then comes the Rhineland with its vineyards; further south are the Swabian and Franconian Alps, which respectively are relatively near the famous Black Forest in the west and the Bavarian and Bohemian Forests in the east; finally we reach the foothills of the Alps in Bavaria, made all the more picturesque by the nearby lakes. Geographically Germany has everything to offer: forests, lakes and mountains with fairy-tale castles, country inns and farm houses to go with the scenery – a tourist Mecca in the *Wirtschaftswunderland*.

One can see much of the country on a morning flight from Heathrow to Frankfurt, and from there by the DLT small propeller planes to the south.

Germany is not only politically divided between West and East by the Iron Curtain, but regionally within the Federal Republic, for historical reasons. West Germany is essentially a collection of regions roughly represented by the different *Länder*, and though the latter work together as a team with no little economic success, the average German tends to identify himself far more strongly with his region than with the country as a whole. Coping with Germany is therefore coping with the particular region or regions one has chosen to visit.

# Preparations and how to get there

The first step is to work out how to get there and the priorities of comfort, speed and economy involved. On these depend whether one travels by road (and sea), rail or air; whether one shops around for package deals with transport and accommodation included or decides to be a loner. It depends upon purse and temperament. Travel offers change frequently and so do fares. Obviously your travel agent or local automobile organization should be able to help with hints and a wealth of brochures to study. Travel within Germany is dealt with in the next chapter

**Planning**

Obviously, going by car takes longer and is more tiring than travelling by rail or air. To save time on the sea crossing (for example the Dover–Ostend crossing takes three hours), it helps to go by Hovercraft in 35 minutes from Dover to Calais and then drive across France and Belgium and Aachen and from there on to Cologne. It is not advisable to go further south without stopping a night or two because the distance is too far and fatigue sets in so that one is too exhausted to look around and enjoy things.

**Road**

Once in Germany, driving to Berlin along the East German motorway in transit can be an adventure: the state of the road is not always good and there could be a long wait at the frontier post. It is essential to keep to the motorway and not to deviate from it, otherwise one could be fined by the East German police for doing so. It is also advisable not to exceed the speed limit. Sometimes the sign-posting is confusing, so it is well worth obtaining detailed routing schedules from the AA or RAC. A Green Card for

*Driving to Berlin*

insurance should also be taken, as well as the log book. See the chapter on East Germany for more detailed advice.

*Driving: take it easy!* Some accident statistics should urge caution and chill the enthusiasm of the racer driver: there are four accidents every minute, somebody injured every minute and somebody killed every hour. Every twelve minutes a child is killed or injured. The main cause of accidents is what the Germans call *Raserei* (tearing along regardless). Or one could put it another way: impatience, fed by fast cars and traffic hold-ups which make drivers throw caution to the winds.

It is also reported that a Japanese automobile manufacturer test drives new sports models on the motorways at speeds of up to 300 kmph, importing cars specially for the purpose. West Germany is the only country in Europe where there is no general speed limit on the motorways.

There is however a *Richtgeschwindigkeit*, that is, a recommended top speed of 130 kmph, but it is not obligatory.

**Rail** Travelling by rail is usually appreciably cheaper, but first of all let us consider the different types of train, which are graded according to speed and comfort.

The grades are: S (suburban local trains); E (semi-fast), i.e. dead slow, stopping at most stations; D (express with supplementary charges for distances up to 50 km); FD (long-distance express, where tickets up to 50 km and season tickets are subject to payment of a supplement); IC (inter-city 'National High-Speed Train', where a supplement is payable which, to quote the timetable, 'comprises the reservation charge. For groups the reservation of seats is necessary'); EC (Euro-City, 'European High-Speed Trains', where supplementary charges are also payable).

The Federal Railways provide sleepers and couchettes, single or double in first class, and with two or three beds in second. Cheaper couchettes are provided in carriages with six beds. These services are provided on the main lines. There are also long-distance train services where cars can be loaded on as well.

There are different routes by train from the UK to Germany. The most usual are Victoria station – Dover – Ostend – Cologne, and Liverpool Street station – Harwich – Hook of Holland – Cologne, and then on south or branch off before Cologne. The advantage of travelling by train this way is that one can enjoy a good night's sleep on the boat and a restful journey on the train the next morning. If going on to the south one can change trains at Cologne, which gives one an hour to visit the cathedral and museum which are only across the road from the railway station.

One of the joys of travelling by train in Germany is that the main stations are often situated in the centre of the cities so that one can reach tourist attractions within a few minutes of alighting from the train. Main stations cater for tourists with information counters (*Auskunft*) and above all *Zimmernachweis* (offices booking accommodation in hotels or cheaper *Pensionen*). These booking facilities are also open at night.

For those interested in steam trains there are special trips to the Transport Museum at Nuremberg or to the Railway Museum at Wirsberg.

*Steam trains*

Pensioners have a special deal when visiting Germany. A pensioner's annual rail pass entitles the holder to up to 50 per cent reduction on rail tickets within the Federal Republic. There are also special pensioners' rates to Germany. If you want to travel first class, you can use your pensioner's rail pass to obtain a corresponding reduction.

*Concessionary fares, rail passes, etc.*

For other travellers there are many different ways of saving on rail fares by travelling on certain weekdays or utilizing special long-distance bargain returns. It pays to try to master the German system of computing fares, which is based on a flat rate per kilometre. If you know how far you want to travel, you can usually calculate the fare yourself.

For those coming to Germany from further afield than the UK it certainly pays to invest in the Eurail Pass, which enables one to travel unlimited distances throughout Europe, excluding the United Kingdom and the Irish Republic. There are different prices according to the length of one's stay. Visiting Germany certainly lends itself to extending one's programme to include neighbouring countries as well.

*Cheaper travel to Berlin*   For political reasons travel to Berlin by air and rail is subsidized, by rail 33⅓ per cent and by air within the Federal Republic also about a third cheaper.

**Air**   Many air travellers shop around for cheapies first, others look for package tours with accommodation included and yet others think of comfort en route to ensure being rested on arrival. All these different requirements demand research. Unfortunately it is outside the scope of this book to give detailed advice, though useful addresses are given at the end of the book. However, it is always best to ask among people who have been to Germany before and enquire at a number of travel agents. It also pays to ring up the individual air companies.

It helps to establish one's priorities. These tend to establish themselves according to one's age and pocket. Usually the senior citizen wants more comfort than the younger traveller, although pensioners often do not have large sums at their disposal and so many have to go tourist or economy class.

While cheaper flights mean less room, fewer WCs on board and in general less comfort, they can still be made less tiring by resting up *before* flying. There is a whole branch of medicine devoted to reducing stress and fatigue in flight. It is also a good idea to have the travel agent enter your phone number with your booking in the computer so that, in theory at least, the airline can call you if the flight is delayed or cancelled. The best thing is to ring the air company's airport office early on the day of departure to enquire if the flight is likely to depart on time.

The main problem for American visitors is that

often one misses a full night's sleep on the plane and usually arrives in the early morning in Germany feeling like a zombie. It is therefore advisable to go straight to a hotel and rest before dashing off to start one's tour.

The principal West German airports are: Frankfurt, *Airports* Munich, Hamburg, Cologne-Bonn, Stuttgart, Berlin-Tegel and Düsseldorf. Frankfurt is enormous, with an average of 400 flights daily and long walks to catch some planes, only partially eased by moving walkways. Crowds can build up at security, so it is advisable to be punctual checking in. If you are in transit for a few hours and are not travelling first class, and thus are not able to use first-class lounges, then go over the bridge to the Sheraton Hotel, where one can sit in comfort and order drinks. The washroom is clean and an oasis of peace compared to the facilities available in the airport itself. Beverages are not cheap, but the extra comfort is worth it and the airport snack counters and restaurants are not cheap either. Please remember that the hotel phones are very expensive. Do use the public phones instead, which are situated in the lobby.

For those who wish to relax before or after a long flight and be alone with their thoughts, there is always the charming little airport chapel to visit. It is interdenominational and has been presented with a Madonna as a 'Nachempfindung der Frankfurter Madonna von Tilman Riemenschneider' (reinterpretation of Tilman Riemenschneider's Frankfurt Madonna). The face of the Madonna represents the young artist's late wife who was killed in a car accident while he was sculpting the statue.

Frankfurt is an airport which does take getting used to. Although parking facilities are conveniently situated under the airport, it is a little confusing finding them and you should always make a careful mental and physical note of where you have left your car. Unfortunately one is not supposed to take luggage trolleys from the door of the garage to one's car. This can be very inconvenient with heavy luggage. It is always best to insist on heavy luggage being checked through to the final point of destination if one is only passing through Frankfurt. One saves considerable toing and froing and time at customs.

On the return flight it always pays to check luggage in early to ensure a choice of seats and freedom from baggage. Trolleys are free. In Munich they are hired out for a fee of DM 1. This can be inconvenient if one does not have any local small change. Airport banks are usually open, but exchanging money wastes time when one is usually tired and anxious to get to one's hotel.

**The language**

How should one go about preparing a trip to Germany? Even given that most Germans, even the least educated, have some English, it does no harm to take an introductory German language course as a sensible form of preparation. Of course one cannot hope to learn to speak fluently in a short time, but at least one can be introduced to the sound of the language. It is not all so harsh and military sounding as one may have been led to believe. It is also a language of great poetry.

Depending upon the quality of the teacher and the size of the class, it should be possible to learn a few words and at least to be able to understand simple sentences in the language. By learning the language one should also become acquainted with everyday situations, such as shopping, being in a train or tram or at the petrol station. Practising everyday situations serves as an excellent introduction to the language and to the country and its people. The Goethe Institute in London (roughly equivalent to the British Council) runs German language courses. There are also Goethe Institutes in America. Another possible introduction to the language would be to listen to German language cassettes in one's car. Glancing through German magazines would help too.

**Entry formalities**

It is essential to be clear on health, immigration (visa) and customs requirements. No inoculations are required, but it is worth remembering that there is rabies in the border areas and the appropriate precautions should be taken. Visas are not usually required for visitors staying up to three months (in the Federal Republic). Citizens of non-Common Market countries require work permits, though normally this would not be relevant to those only staying for a short time. Usually teachers do not require work permits. Customs requirements are more stringent in regard to importing coffee and tea than in other countries. Both items attract duty above a minimal limit because they are costly in Germany. Pets and animals with the appropriate health certificates may be brought into the country and do not have to be placed in quarantine as in the United Kingdom.

Visitors are required to register arrival and place of sojourn with the municipality. Hotels merely require their guests to complete registration forms which are then handed to the police daily. I remember staying in a *Pension* in Munich, and a policeman calling to collect the registration forms at two o'clock in the morning! If staying privately, the host or hostess is supposed to inform the authorities. Obviously campers cannot do this at every night stop, but, when staying in a place for a longer than a few days, one is expected to report to the municipal aliens department (*Ordnungsamt*) to which Germans, when moving place of residence, are also required to report. The visitor is advised to take this formality seriously and thus not run foul of local officialdom. It should be remembered that all German citizens are required to have identity cards and are expected to carry them on their persons at all times. Even drunken vagabonds will be asked to produce their identity cards! So visitors are always expected to carry their passports as proof of identity. Woe betide the unfortunate who is unable to satisfy the demand, 'Ihr (Reise)pass, bitte.'

*East Berlin*

All nationalities are welcome there, but an exception is made when it is suspected that individual travellers from certain countries are trying to enter the Federal Republic on false pretences via East Berlin. Recently there has been a large number of people claiming refugee status (i.e. that they were persecuted at home), whereas this was seen by the authorities as a bogus excuse to improve their economic position by being supported as refugees in a richer country than their own. From West Berlin it is very easy to visit East Berlin. (For entry formalities into East Germany proper, see the chapter on East Germany.)

# Travel within Germany

One has to decide whether one wants to see as much as possible in the time available or a little in detail. As a tourist, I always prefer to concentrate on one place first to get the feel of a new country before doing the grand tour, which is usually exhausting and superficial.

**Students and young people**

Students should not forget to take their student cards (*Studentenausweise*) or better still, obtain an international student card. There are many worthwhile travel reductions available for students, and also cheap accommodation at *Jugendherbergen* (youth hostels).

Women, particularly, should exercise great care when hitch-hiking. Bloody murders have occurred. (See the advice given to motorists on picking up hitch-hikers later in the chapter.) A safer alternative to hitch-hiking is to use the *Mitfahrzentrale*, an agency which has branches in major towns throughout the country. For a small fee, it puts people wanting lifts in touch with drivers offering them; passengers contribute towards expenses.

**Flying**

A large disadvantage for foreign visitors to the Federal Republic is that there is no round ticket available for air travel around the country, as there is in Australia, the United States and in South Africa. Those on a budget should try to take return tickets over a weekend: supposing one is based in Munich and wants to spend the weekend in Hamburg, as long as Saturday night is included there one can fly for half the normal return fare and return at any time. The ticket is usually valid for three months for inland and six months for foreign flights. If you book two weeks or more in advance the fare is even cheaper.

Assuming you have decided to concentrate on

visiting Germany but would not be averse to visiting England as well, then again the weekend offers are very tempting. The absurd thing is that it is cheaper to buy a weekend return flight from Munich to London than a normal return flight from Munich to Hamburg.

It is worth noting for British visitors that it is much cheaper to book return flights from Britain than from Germany and that, once resident or stationed in Germany, it pays to book and pay for tickets with a British travel agent, or with the London office of Lufthansa or British Airways.

**Rail travel**     Travelling by train is an experience. The first impression is usually of smart-looking railway officials clad in a variety of uniforms, with a special man responsible for the departure of the train. He wears a red sash and carries a whistle at the ready. At main terminals there is normally an official wearing a hat with '*Auskunft*' (information) emblazoned across it. He usually carries an enormous timetable and is both knowledgeable and helpful.

Every platform should have lists of arrivals (*Ankunft*) and departures (*Abfahrt*) showing the time (*Uhrzeit*) based on a 24-hour clock, the *Bahngleis* (platform number) and the main destination alongside the intermediary stations, with an arrow pointing to connecting trains.

Trains are punctual, clean and comfortable, but they have high steps, and for the elderly considerable agility is required to get on and care to alight. Porters are seldom present, so trolleys are at hand. Although the heating can be overpowering, it can be regulated. There is a supplement to pay on the TEE (Trans European Express) trains, but it is worth it. It is superb travel, but snacks are expensive, so it does pay to take sandwiches or eat well beforehand. Trains also run throughout the night, thus offering impecunious travellers a chance to save on accommodation.

For long transcontinental journeys it is essential to book a seat in advance, which means at the latest the previous day. This especially applies in summer on trains going south to Italy.

*'Even under democracy your trains run on time.'*

**Driving**

Life in Germany without a motor car can be purgatorial, if one has to do much travelling within a short period of time. However good the train and air services, driving a car means being independent. However, there is an art to driving in Germany which is worth mastering.

The main practical problem for visitors of some nationalities is the priority from the right at a crossroads or junction. This does not apply where one road is marked as having priority over another. Once on a roundabout one usually has priority. Where one has to be careful is where priorities change on the roundabout itself.

Signposts are sometimes confusing because they often point *to* but not *in* the direction concerned, and the special blue signs to the motorways do not make directions clear if they are pointing to different motorways. It is the arrow next to the particular motorway sign which one has to watch for.

*Different psychology*

Please remember that Germans on four wheels are different people to when on two feet, and that

German psychology in any case has its own way of functioning. If a German has right of way, he or she will tend to take it regardless of the danger involved, because it is presumed that other drivers will give way. It is often a blind trust in everyone obeying the rules.

Germans tend also to be impatient drivers. They do not like being held up by ditherers. As a visiting motorist it is often impossible to do anything but dither. It therefore pays to go over the route on the map before a day's drive. It also pays to ask at the hotel reception desk exactly how to negotiate the local traffic.

*Turning* When the traffic light is at red, American visitors should not turn right at a junction with a side road. You may only do this if there is a special lane from your road into the side turning which *avoids* the traffic lights. Remember too that when turning into another street at a traffic light, pedestrians have priority crossing the road on their green light, which will be simultaneous with yours. It is unnerving for foreign motorists to see pedestrians cross the road into which one has turned on green. The same dangerous situation occurs when a tram halts at a stop in the centre of the street and the people either alighting or wishing to get on, who have been waiting on the pavement, just walk across the street almost regardless of the traffic which is bearing down upon them. It's a crazy system. The best thing is to be extremely careful when following a tram in a city where the tram stops are not behind protective railings.

One traffic light signal for those turning left across the main stream of traffic is confusing and thus can be most dangerous. It is a green 'go' arrow which lights up. If the light is constant, i.e. does not blink on and off, you may turn left. If it (or a yellow arrow) starts blinking, *do not turn* unless the street is clear of oncoming traffic. The green arrow usually only shines constantly for a short time, when the oncoming traffic is halted by a red light which you of course cannot see. When the yellow arrow blinks, it means that you may turn if there is no oncoming traffic. Even experienced motorists are confused, and sometimes the system of allowing one to turn left across the main stream of traffic varies from city to city. One has to be very careful when turning left in traffic. Again, German drivers know their traffic code and assume everybody else does too. They tend to insist on their rights in traffic even though this could, and sometimes does, lead to an accident. Strange, but true.

*Towing*

Those who tow caravans should remember that it is strictly forbidden for passengers to travel in the caravan whilst it is being towed.

*Driving on motorways*

Driving on the motorway (*Autobahn*) requires quicker reflexes than in English-speaking countries with speed limits. A recent campaign by environmentalists to impose a speed limit failed. When accidents occur, they are usually catastrophic. Visitors are warned not to drive when tired, to keep off the extreme left lane except when overtaking and every now and again to slow down and use the extreme right lane rather than hog the middle one and fall asleep, which some people do with tragic results. Great care should be taken on entering an *Autobahn*. People do occasionally drive down the wrong side of the motorway; they are called appropriately enough *Geisterfahrer* (ghost drivers). If you do have or become involved in an accident, do all you can to get your vehicle on to the emergency shoulder and out of the traffic. Place your warning sign (in Germany a triangle) 150 metres back towards the oncoming traffic and do this at the double. The initial accident is often not nearly as serious as the subsequent ones caused by fast unwarned car drivers crashing at Nuremberg-Ring speeds into stationary cars blocking the motorway. Then stay on the verge: many people lose their lives by being mown down from behind.

It cannot be emphasized too much that quick thinking and reactions on the *Autobahn* are essential. If you are tired, do stop and have a rest, get some exercise and try to relax. This is all so obvious, but British and American drivers do not realize how fast traffic moves on motorways with no speed limit. Whilst one does not have to worry unduly about driving in Germany, one does have to be careful!

*Watch out for official holidays*

The effect of public and school holidays on motorway traffic is obvious, but it is compounded by the fact that many people driving to Austria from the north or returning at the end of their holidays use German motorways in transit. The public holidays are as follows: Epiphany, Shrove Tuesday, Ash Wednesday, Good Friday, Easter Sunday, May Day, Ascension, Whit Sunday, Whit Monday, Day of German Unity (17 June), Corpus Christi, Harvest Festival, All Souls' Day, All Saints' Day, Day of Prayer and Repentance (16 November).

The main traffic problem is during the summer months. School holidays in West Germany have been staggered according to the different *Länder* in an attempt to spread the holiday traffic, as far as possible, over different periods of the summer. In general it is advisable to avoid weekends, if possible, on the motorways. A little sunshine, more or less any time of the year, will attract a lot of traffic. The worst time to travel is early evening, when everyone returns home.

A major factor in driving in the south is the weather. The Munich–Salzburg motorway, especially popular in summer, can suddenly be submerged in monsoon-like downpours which make a mockery of any but the most robust and smoothly operating windscreen wiper. If you get caught in a downpour, pull into the nearest lay-by or rest area until the rain stops. You should not have to wait long and when you resume your drive it will be much more pleasant and, of course, safer.

*Raststätten*

If you do a lot of driving on the motorways, you will surely stop at a *Raststätte* or *Rasthaus* (service area) to fill up with petrol, wash and have a meal. Whilst they are usually satisfactory, especially the new ones such as Rasthaus Weiskirchen with its tastefully arranged free-flow Restaurant, one can save money by avoiding them and leaving the motorway. It is also much more fun to eat in a village pub.

For readers of German the ADAC (Allgemeiner Deutscher Automobil Club) publishes a book, *Beiderseits der Autobahn* (both sides of the motorway), to help those who want to escape the main stream of traffic for a while. A little map reading and keeping an eye open for interesting and attractive-looking places either side of the *Autobahn* should suffice to find somewhere oneself. Finding the road to a village can be confusing. The place off on the right may only be reachable by leaving the motorway and turning left, doubling back on one's tracks, and then going through a tunnel to reach the right-hand side of the motorway. The golden rule is to follow the signs carefully on leaving the *Autobahn*, even if they appear to be pointing in the wrong direction.

*Picking up hitch-hikers*

The best advice is 'Don't!', even if it wrings your heart to see some young tramp thumbing a lift. Whilst drinking coffee at a *Raststätte* you may be approached by a smooth-talking hitch-hiker. But it is best to refuse, even if he really is a student going back to college or someone genuinely down on his luck and short of money for a train ticket. It could be that the inoffensive young person chatting you up could slit your throat later on; there have been tragic cases in the past. A polite 'Sorry, no', or in German, 'Leider nicht', with a smile, is all that is required.

It is against the law to stop either on the motorway or the special entry lane to it, to give someone a lift. It is not against the law to agree to take someone at a *Raststätte*, but you have been warned. The other complication is that in the event of having an accident, you could be liable to your passenger or his parents for all expenses.

In case this seems too heartless, please remember that German students have many opportunities open to them for cheap travel, through their student travel offices, the Federal Railways bus companies, or the *Mitfahrzentrale*.

*Don't drink and drive!* It goes without saying that one should *not* drive after having a few drinks. If caught by the police, who are empowered to require a driver to blow into a breathalyser, one is liable to have one's driving licence confiscated on the spot. If one has an accident, the insurance will probably disclaim all responsibility for settling the claim.

The Federal police are entitled to treat foreign drivers according to local laws, though foreign service-men may simply be handed over to their respective military police. If you drink and drive there are distinctions in how the police will treat you, according to the circumstances. If you are simply stopped by the police and are found to have driven up to 0.79 *Promille* (79 millilitres; concentration of alcohol in the blood), nothing will happen; if, however, one is involved in an accident, then one could have one's licence taken away (*Fahrscheinentzug*) (for Germans up to nine months) and have to leave the car where it was, assuming of course that it is drivable. If Germans are caught having drunk 0.8 to 1.29 *Promille*, they have four points marked against them in the 'sinners' catalogue' (*Bußkatalog*) at Flensburg, even if they have driven faultlessly, and will have their licences taken away for at least one month. If they repeat the offence, they can be forbidden to drive for three months (*Fahrverbot*). There is a distinction between having one's licence taken away from one and being forbidden to drive. With the former one receives the licence back automatically. With the latter one has to reapply for a licence at the end of the period for which it was originally withdrawn. With over 1.3 *Promille* in one's blood, regardless of whether one is driving correctly or not, the licence is withdrawn for a minimum of nine months and there is a hefty fine as well. A higher *Promille* in the blood leads to a higher fine and where the alcohol content is very high, the judge can require the driver to undergo a special psychological test. The police are particularly on the lookout for those driving under the influence of alcohol.

However, it is not only self-discipline that is *Take a taxi!*
required, but extreme caution during the beer festivals at night. Although the police constantly advise
those attending to use taxis as opposed to driving
their own cars, some beer enthusiasts still risk driving
when intoxicated, and very nasty accidents occur.
Often it really is simpler, when going out at night to
dinner or to the theatre, to disregard the additional
expense and to go and return by taxi (or minicab
which is cheaper in the large cities). There is nothing
worse than trying to find a place to park in a large
German city. There are of course large parking
garages (*Parkhäuser*) available, but one needs to find
out where they are beforehand and it could be that
when one arrives, they are full. Moreover, they are
not cheap.

The police may levy a so-called *Verwarnungsgeld* (up *Police fines*
to DM 40) for speeding or causing an accident or
simply disregarding a traffic regulation. One can
refuse to pay and appear in court, but it is wiser to
pay up to save time, a possibly increased fine and
court costs. (See the same subject dealt with in the
chapter on East Germany.) Above all, one wants to
avoid a traffic policeman confiscating one's driving
licence (say for having drunk over the limit) and
forbidding one to drive further. Usually policemen
are very understanding with foreigners but, as one
says, 'auch sie sind nur Menschen' (they are only
human).

Here even greater caution is called for, not only from *Mopeds*
the moped rider, but especially from the motorist.
Again, having seen so many accidents, it is difficult
not to become a kill-joy. In theory moped riders
should wear helmets, but many of them do not.
Motor cyclists have to, but again some do not. All
one can advise a visiting motorist, not familiar with
local traffic conditions, is to exercise the utmost care.

**Using public transport – coping with buses and trams**

When visiting a large city or even a small town, considerable money on taxis can be saved by mastering the public transport system which usually, unlike in London or Los Angeles, works efficiently.

Munich, Frankfurt, Hamburg and Berlin have their own underground railways. As with the trams, which still run in those cities, and some buses, one is required to buy tickets or blocks of them (cheaper than single ones) *before* getting on and then cancelling the ticket in a special machine on the underground train, tram or bus in question. Failure to do so can render one liable to payment of a fine. *Schwarzfahrer* (non-payers) are not appreciated.

If uncertain, always ask for assistance; usually someone will understand the problem and help. With trams and buses, it is essential to get in at the *Einstieg* (entrance) and alight at the *Ausstieg* (exit) behind. Otherwise one causes consternation. Trying to board a bus at the exit in the rush-hour will not promote international friendship. You may not understand what is being said, but the tone of voice will be unmistakably hostile. It is better not to try the public transport system out during the rush-hour (7–8 a.m. and 4.30–6.30 p.m.), when it is everyone for themselves. It pays to keep off people's corns and get off the bus quickly. Near the destination start to edge towards the exit and then be prepared to alight quickly when it is reached. A German girl-friend of mine was not quick enough alighting from a Munich tram and had to leave a shoe behind and then hobble home!

Queuing in Germany is often nonexistent. People tend to storm buses rather than wait meekly in an orderly line. British patience and phlegm are out of place. When you get on, watch out for those seats specially reserved for invalids. They are marked with a sort of skull and crossbones, and it is extraordinary how Long-John-Silver-like an otherwise meek-looking disabled passenger can become if one inadvertently occupies his seat and then does not surrender it immediately when that person produces his invalid identity card. (In any brush with an outraged local or official, prudence is *always* the

better part of valour – a smile of contrition and a
meek gesture and you will be excused. Stop and argue
and you are lost.)

Once you have mastered the technique, you will
find going by public transport rewarding. You see the
people at close quarters and are forced to communi-
cate with them. You are more of a visitor and less of a
tourist.

Bicycles may be rented at some railway stations and **Bicycles**
can be returned to others along the line. It costs either
DM 5 or DM 10 per day, depending upon whether
one has a ticket or not. There is no deposit to pay, but
one is required to show one's passport. A word of
warning is due. Although special cycle tracks are now
provided in most towns, many of them on the
pavements are dangerous for pedestrians. There are
still far too many accidents to make cycling anything
but hazardous. Although there are speed limits in
built-up areas and the police do all they can to enforce
them, 60 kilometres per hour seems very slow to most
drivers. Sometimes too, the crossings for cyclists onto
the roadway are confusing for both parties.

For those staying for a few months, Germany makes **Travel**
a very good starting-off point for short visits to **elsewhere**
neighbouring countries. From Munich one can visit
Salzburg, from Freiburg Basel, from Aachen the
Benelux countries and from Flensburg Scandinavia.
From Bavarian border towns one can go on bus
excursions to Prague. One can manage a lot in a
weekend and it seems a pity not to avail oneself of the
opportunity.

A further possibility for those interested in going
on pilgrimages are the various *Pilgerfahrten* offered
by local travel agents.

# Where to stay

Germany is a tourist's Mecca: castles, lakes, forests, rivers and mountains. A rich variety of accommodation is offered, ranging from luxury hotels down the scale to simple *Pensionen,* which in Germany have the saving grace of always being clean. There is also an excellent collection of rented houses and accommodation throughout the country (see the chapter on Living Accommodation).

**Hotels, bed and breakfast** Travel agents will advise on hotels, Lufthansa publishes a list, the red Michelin guide book is very comprehensive and for the last-minute visitor, every small town seems to have a *Verkehrsamt* (tourist office) or some form of *Zimmernachweis* (booking agency) which has a list of hotels and *Pensionen* in the more moderate price range. Large railway stations like Munich are very well organized in this respect. They are in any case fascinating places to explore, together with their book shops, restaurants and groceries, and in summer you can see young people camped on the floor!

Motorists can of course look for private houses with the sign *Zimmer frei* (room free) or *Fremdenzimmer* (visitors' accommodation). Such notices abound in tourist areas, particularly in mountain villages. One is usually assured of a clean bed and a friendly welcome.

*Asking the price* It is as well to ask the price first, and whether it is *alles inklusiv/inbegriffen* (everything included: local taxes and of course breakfast), to avoid an unpleasant surprise next morning.

*Extras* Breakfast is usually included (*Frühstück inbegriffen*), but it is as well to enquire. Breakfast may or may not include an egg (*Ei*) or (one has to be careful) cold meats (*Wurst*). Germans are very commercial and one may be asked if one wants cold meats and, thinking it is included, find it is an extra popped on the bill.

*Always ask first*

It is always advisable when obtaining any product or service in Germany to ask *beforehand* what the price is. One then knows exactly what to pay. Always ask for the *Endsumme* (the final cost). The first figure quoted may be appreciably less than the final one. Have no inhibitions about asking before. It is in no way taken exception to. It is not a bad idea to pay one night in advance to establish confidence. Ask for a receipt. Then one is sure that one has understood the price. Nothing mars a business relationship more – however short – than misunderstanding. For those who are on a fairly tight budget, getting things straight first helps considerably.

*Telephones*

It is well worth avoiding using the telephone in hotels if one is price conscious. Each unit could be DM 1 or 50 Pfennigs as opposed to the Post Office rate of 23 Pfennigs. Hotels usually have one or more pay phones, and it will save a lot of money if one takes the trouble to use them. If one is going to do a lot of telephoning, it is as well to ascertain how much the hotel charges for a unit. This should be stated in writing on a notice next to the telephone, but if it is not, do enquire at reception. You will be surprised how expensive calls can be.

**Self-catering**

Self-catering is very well organized in Germany, and the German National Tourist Board issues a comprehensive brochure on the subject giving all details and explaining booking arrangements and the cost involved. The choice is extensive, the pictures of chalets, villas and apartments mouthwatering. Having decided on which type of accommodation is best suited to individual or family needs, the next thing is to decide on the sort of place one wants to visit: a small country town (one finds them all over Germany), a village, near water (a lake, river, at the seaside) or in the mountains. One has to decide on the region: Hamburg and the North Sea (*Nordsee*) or Bavaria (mountains, lakes and Munich), Franconia (mountains, scenery, castles and Nuremberg) or Berlin (divided city, Iron Curtain, *Third Man* atmosphere).

**Motor homes**     A variation on the usual forms of accommodation would be to hire a so-called motor home, with optional extras including even a telephone. This can work out fairly expensive; to the basic hire and mileage charges should be added the deposit, collision damage waiver, personal accident insurance, petrol, German VAT at 14 per cent and other necessities such as camping guide, propane, fresh water, toilet chemicals (where used) and final cleaning. Obviously this sort of travel is for the initiated and entails assuming more responsibility than many holiday makers would be prepared for.

# Food and drink

To call Germany a country of sausage eaters is exaggerating. Mercifully sausage is not the sole diet. Moreover, there are so many different types of sausage, some eaten warm, others cold; some in the north, others in the south; sometimes with every region, even a city, having its own special sausage. For visitors in need of a quick, tasty and relatively cheap snack, sausage is ideal, sold as it is in butcher's shops and at kiosks as well as in the classier restaurants. Even Queen Victoria and recently Princess Margaret, whilst on a visit to Coburg, sent for hot sausages from the kiosk on the market-place near the gates of the Ducal Palace and, by all accounts, enjoyed eating them.

Eating and drinking is a national occupation. There is nothing rushed about cooking and eating food or drinking wine; people eat with deliberation and drink with distinction. Here it is necessary to distinguish between restaurant and kiosk or fast food, between a sit-down meal or a stand-up snack. The latter is particularly useful for tourists who are short of money and time.

German cuisine is superb for the hungry, but the best cooking is French. Gourmets will be satisfied too, but with the £ at around DM 3, it is an expensive pastime. For weight watchers it will be a losing battle. German cooking is based on the oven and the frying pan and is full of fat and cholesterol. It tastes excellent, especially when wine is included.

**Restaurants**

On entering a restaurant with a German lady it is, unlike in English-speaking countries, the gentleman who goes in first to ensure that everything is in order for the lady to enter. When having lunch or dinner in a restaurant, it is often a good idea to choose one of the *Gedecke* or the *Menü*. These are a combined meal (soup, main course and pudding) which is usually cheaper than if one ordered the courses separately. The menu is just a single combined meal. Choosing *Gedecke* or the *Menü* has the advantage of ensuring one is served quickly.

*Soups*  German soups are tasty and filling, especially *Gulaschsuppe* in the south, and *Ochsenschwanzsuppe* (oxtail) in the north, as well as bread soup. Goulash soup often serves as a snack on its own.

*Meat*  Meat is cooked differently. There is seldom roast beef for lunch. The equivalent (*Roastbeef*) is usually served cold. *Schweinebraten* (roast pork) tastes different to the British variety because of the different cattle feed, different way the meat is cut up after slaughter and different method of cooking. German cooks add water to the meat whilst it is in the oven.

*Puddings*  German puddings (*Nachtische*) are not very good, with the exception of *Apfelstrudel* which, served with cream, makes a real delicacy. Soups and entrées are so filling that there is often very little room left for puddings or dessert. One is just grateful to sit quietly and drink coffee. There is usually an Italian ice cream parlour nearby where children and the sweet-toothed can indulge themselves.

*Bread*  Rolls, called *Semmel* in South Germany and *Brötchen* in the north, are usually eaten at breakfast, though they can be eaten at other meals as well, particularly with soup or sausages. Helpings are so large (especially when *Knödel* (dumplings) are on the menu) that one has no need of bread or rolls as a filler.

Bread is not just a staple food but almost a delicacy as well, in the sense that there are so many different kinds of bread to go with different courses, and to be eaten on different occasions. Go into a good bakery (and most of them are) and you will be confronted by a profusion of different types of bread.

*Toothpicks*  Toothpicks are available in restaurants and there is an art in using them by covering the instrument with one's hand while excavating in the dental cavities.

Tipping is always an art, especially today when the tipped may be earning more than the tipper. In Germany waiters and waitresses are paid a relatively low basic wage and are also entitled to ten per cent of the bill, which may, in the more exclusive restaurants, be noted on the bill as such (*Bedienung*). Or, which is now frequently the practice, the ten per cent is included in the prices on the menu (*Speisekarte*). These prices also include VAT (*Mehrwertsteuer*). *Tips*

    The ten per cent service charge represents in effect the waiters' and waitresses' wages. It is *not* therefore a gratuity, although visitors from English-speaking countries may be inclined to regard it as such. Over and above the service charge, one is expected to add a few Pfennigs to the bill at the end. If it came to DM 10.20, then one would either make it DM 10.50 or, if one were especially pleased with the service, DM 11; if DM 96, one would normally make it DM 100. One does not have to do this; eyebrows might be raised if one does not, but nobody will say anything.

In restaurants and cafés waitresses and waiters adopt a special mode of speech, just as shop assistants do: 'Was darf es sein?' ('What may I bring (or sell) you?'). To call a waiter you say 'Herr Ober!' or a waitress 'Fräulein!' (Miss, even if she is obviously a married woman of advanced age); the answer may well be: 'Ich komme gleich' (I'm coming soon) or 'Ich komme sofort' (I'm coming immediately), and he or she does not. In time one learns that when people say they are going to attend to you immediately, they usually take their time! The best thing to do either in a restaurant or café is to fetch a newspaper to read or go to the loo. The worst thing one can do is to lose one's temper or become impatient. All that will happen is that you will hear more promises, this time monosyllabic, but louder: 'Gleich!' or 'Sofort'; yet one thing you can be sure of is that no one will come. Undoubtedly the best approach is to look as though you have all the *Getting served*

time in the world, even if you have not; then someone
is sure to bustle up to you!

**Eating
reasonably
and cheaply**  If you want a reasonably priced meal in a restaurant,
you can go to a 'Wienerwald' restaurant in South
Germany and eat grilled chicken or a 'Nordsee'
restaurant in the north and eat fish (both large chains
of restaurants). However, it is often better to take the
time to seek out a small family restaurant, where the
meal will usually taste better and the price be even
more moderate. Italian pizzerias also provide excellent quick and reasonably priced meals with fresh
salads.

For quick meals and snacks, one can eat very
reasonably in *Steh-Imbißstuben* (kiosks where you
eat standing up), which serve *Schaschlik* (kebabs).
different varieties of hot and cold sausage and other
snacks. Or one can usually find a butcher's shop
where *warmer Leberkäse* (warm meat loaf),
*Schweinebraten* (pork cooked the German way) or
grilled chicken are sold. One can buy rolls and soft
drinks too. Assistants at the meat counters in
supermarkets are used to preparing rolls with meat,
ham or sausage inside, and will sometimes be able to
add pickled cucumber to make the rolls even tastier.
Take-away salads are also available. McDonald's
restaurants are to be found all over Germany, with
Kentucky Fried Chicken muscling in.

**Wines**  One of the glories of staying in Germany is sampling
the wine. Everyone has a favourite wine: some prefer
*Rheingau*, others *Rheinhessen* or *Frankenwein* (produced around Würzburg). Many concentrate on
*Spätlese*, yet others choose wine from the leading
growers such as Dr Bürklin-Wolf in the Rheinpfalz
or Schloss Eltz in the Rheingau, while some rely on
the type of grape: Riesling, Sylvaner and Müller-
Thurgau. More down-market wines such as *Mosel-
tröpfchen* or *Liebfrauenmilch* satisfy many palates
too. Supermarkets often have special offers. You can
buy a bottle of wine for a few Marks upwards, to
about DM 300 for a *Trockenbeerenauslese*. For those
who are particularly interested in wine tasting, one

could recommend the special Moselle cruises down the river from Koblenz to Trier, or even 'The Floating Wine Seminar' in the autumn from Cologne to Basle. Both are arranged by the KD German Rhine Line.

Cheaper wines are also imported from Austria, Italy, Hungary and Yugoslavia. The recent wine scandal emanating from Austria and Italy, featuring the inclusion of Glycol (antifreeze mixture) in wine, scared everybody. Things have now returned to normal.

Knowing some of the terms used to classify wine may help to get better value out of the wine list if the waiter or waitress is not able to advise you. Obviously the wine waiter in the better sort of restaurant should be able to help. It is certainly not necessary to choose the most expensive wine and there may be a perfectly adequate *Hauswein* (house wine) or local wine, or one can simply ask for a glass of 'offenen Wein', that is, for a glass of wine, white or red.

*Wine classification*

The two most vital terms are *süß* (sweet) and *trocken* (dry). The wine, or the grape from which it is made, is classified according to the time of year when harvested. This determines the ripeness, quality and sweetness of the grape. To begin with there is ordinary *Tafelwein* (table wine) and *Landwein* (wine of the region); both are nothing special – the former sweet, the latter dryer. Then there is the so-called *Qualitätswein*, still ordinary wine but officially tested and having a certain character.

Next follow the superior *Qualitätsweine mit Prädikat*, which include (in order of increasing superiority): *Kabinett, Spätlese*, harvested two weeks later than the normal wine and thus sweeter because it has enjoyed more sun; *Auslese,* made from the fully ripened healthy grape picked during the harvest in late summer when the grape is neither too sweet nor too sour; *Beerenauslese*, made from specially selected grapes; *Trockenbeerenauslese*, normally very sweet and the most expensive; and finally *Eiswein*, which is fairly rare and is harvested after the first frost in

November and is normally the sweetest of all, depending upon how much sun the grapes get.

Be careful of *Federweisser* which is young, not fully matured wine which tastes wonderful but can cause stomach upset. Most German wines are white, though there are some very drinkable red-graped rosé wines (*Portugieser Weissherbst* and *Württemberger Trollinger*, for example).

As a young German connoisseur, Alexander Ross, says, 'You see what you get.' The label illustrated shows: 1) the vintage year; 2) the legal definition of area and sub-area; 3) the type of grape; 4) the *Prädikat*; 5) the wine-growing region; 6) the winery, i.e. where the bottle was filled. (Individual wine growers combine to have their wine bottled individually under their own respective labels by a central winery.)

*Schnaps*  Austrian and German *Schnaps* is much more potent

Information on a German wine label
Reproduced by courtesy of Joseph Graf von Montgelas Weinkellerei GmbH, Bingen am Rhein

than French liqueur and is swallowed down in one or two gulps whilst drinking beer. *Unterberg* and *Jägermeister* are referred to as 'medicine' for the stomach.

Pubs are open from morning till night, including Sunday. This favours the custom of enjoying the *Frühschoppen*, which means having a drink between ten and twelve on Sunday morning before lunch. There are also discussions on television at this time, when commentators and experts debate the news over a glass of wine.  *Frühschoppen*

For a non-alcoholic drink, one cannot recommend the local *Apfelsaft* (apple juice) or *Traubensaft* (grape juice) too highly. There is no equivalent of English cider, but Frankfurters are justifiably proud of their *Ebbelwei* (apple wine).  **Other drinks**

Beer is a national drink which comes in many different shades and tastes – over 5000 different kinds are produced by 1200 breweries. It is famous for its purity, being brewed according to a law laid down by Duke Heinrich of Bavaria in 1516 restricting brewers to the use of four ingredients: malted barley, hops, yeast and water. The only permissible exception is to use wheat for the celebrated *Weizen* (wheat) beers of Bavaria. There has recently been lively debate in Brussels between West Germany and other members of the European Community about the Bavarian *Reinheitsgebot* (purity law).  **Beer**

The two main types of beer are divided between the *ober-* and *untergärig*, that is, the top and bottom-fermented beers. The former include *Kölsch* from Cologne, *Altbier* from the lower Rhein, *Dampf Bier*, brewed by the Meisel Brothers in Bayreuth, and the *Weissbiere* from Bavaria. The latter include *Pilsner* or *Pils*, *Export*, *Helles-* and *Dunkelesbier*, *Festbiere* (*Weihnachts-*, *Osterfests-*, *Oktoberfests-* and *allgemeine Volksfestsbiere*, that is, stronger beer which is brewed for special seasonal occasions),

*Bockbier* and *Doppelbockbier*. For those who wish to avoid alcohol there are alcohol-free beers.

In Upper Franconia there are many small breweries which produce their own varieties of beer. The Meisel Brothers have a brewery museum which is quoted in the *Guinness Book of Records* (1988) as being 'the most comprehensive Beer Museum'.

In Bavaria beer is the regional drink and regarded as part of a *normal* citizen's life. Beer is thus not regarded as a *Genussmittel* (luxury), but as a *Nahrungsmittel* (nourishment), although enjoyment and duty seem to go hand in hand. When beer is served the waiter or waitress will always say 'Zum Wohl' or 'Wohl bekomm's', which is the equivalent of 'Your good health' or 'Cheers'. The waitress will usually put the corresponding number of marks or strokes on your beer mat.

There is of course a whole culture attached to beer mugs, not so much the kitsch sold to tourists, but the normal coloured ones which patrons keep at their locals on special hooks, especially the Fayancen, the extremely valuable Creussener, and other antique mugs.

**Beer gardens and beer halls**

A traditional way of spending the evening with friends in the summer is to go to a *Biergarten*. Visitors may enjoy the experience as well. At the back of many pubs there is a garden where patrons sit and enjoy their beer in the open air, and simple food is served as well. Other larger, more elaborate *Biergärten* are to be found in the cities. They prove a welcome change from the *Bierhallen* which are patronized in winter. Munich is a city particularly renowned for its beer halls. Usually in the larger beer halls there is a band playing marches or folk music. It is an acquired taste for some and a more immediately enjoyable experience for others.

**Kaffee-ausschank: a cup of coffee**

Coffee drinking is a national pastime in Germany. It is a pleasant, convivial habit. Coffee, which is now cheaper than it used to be, is almost always filtered and thus has a stronger taste than coffee made in the French way. Coffee beans are sold in packets. One can either grind the beans at home with a coffee mill or have it done in the shop or supermarket.

Coffee *Ausschänke* are excellent places to meet and talk to the man in the street or old-age pensioners with enough time on their hands to chat. One may see a few strange people too, but though they may be eccentric, they should be harmless. A cup of coffee usually costs half what is charged in a café. One collects a cup of coffee from the counter, drinks it standing up at little round tables and then returns it for washing up.

The *Ausschank* also does a roaring trade in a mixed selection of goods (clocks, watches, scarves, even furniture). Some of them are of surprisingly good quality, and much cheaper than in the shops.

**Cafés**

Some of the pleasures of life in Germany cost very little, for example sitting in a café. The nice thing about German cafés is just being able to sit there undisturbed and see the world go by. For those who like to sit and read there is usually a selection of newspapers and magazines to enjoy. The only problem, but one that the Federal Ministers of Health have promised to tackle, is smoke. However, in summer or when the weather allows, it is often possible to sit out in the open.

*Eiskaffee* (iced coffee) is also to be recommended in summer.

**Cakes and pastries**

German cakes are not as sophisticated as French gâteaux, but superbly appetizing all the same, a gourmet's delight and a weight watcher's agony. As with bread, there are many different types of cake, varying with the region.

All over Germany, cafés and *Konditoreien* (cake shops) offer *Obstkuchen* (fruit tart), *Sandkuchen* (roughly like Madeira cake) and in Swabia there is the very tasty *Schwäbischer Apfelkuchen*, which is an apple flan. This is often on sale in the south. The same holds for the delicious *Stachelbeertorte* (gooseberry tart).

Bavaria is the home of the celebrated *Zwetschgendatschi*, made of pastry with damsons (*Zwetschgen*) on top. It is a speciality of Upper Bavaria. In other parts of Bavaria, for example Upper Franconia, *Zwetschgendatschi* made with yeast pastry is sold. *Pflaumenkuchen* is similar, but made with ordinary plums.

More gloriously tasty cakes for the non-weight watcher are the *Schwarzwälder Kirschtorte* (Black Forest gâteau – chocolate cake with cherries, whipped cream and alcohol) and the originally Viennese *Sachertorte*. The *Sachertorte* is a chocolate cake, made originally by an Austrian, Franz Sacher, in Vienna. It is still made by his descendants. When Franz's son Eduard, who had been excluded in his mother's will from the family business, concluded a contract with a bakery and presumed to make and sell the *Sachertorte* without family permission, 25 years' litigation ensued between the father's and son's respective firms or their successors. It became known as the Vienna *Tortenkrieg* (cake battle), ultimately won in the dead father's name.

Another famous confectioner and cake maker is Herr Kreutzkamm from Dresden, who has an elegant café in Munich. Kreutzkamm chocolates are famous the world over and make a welcome present for folk at home.

A speciality of the Advent and Christmas season is the *Lebkuchen*, which originated in fourteenth-century Nuremberg. It is a small biscuit-like cake tasting mainly of cinnamon.

# Living accommodation

Living accommodation in Germany is, like most things, well organized and of good quality. Things usually work, there is efficient central heating, fully equipped kitchens, and often fitted carpets. But how does one rent accommodation apart from the very short-term offers already mentioned?

Advertisements in the paper often provide the answer. Either one answers other people's or inserts one's own. In a very popular city like Munich considerable good fortune and stamina are required. Accordingly it may be easier to settle for a few miles outside. Fast trains (*S-Bahn*) make commuting easy.

Estate agents (*Makler*) can be helpful, but also tricky people to deal with if one has bad luck or simply fails to observe a few simple rules. Never pay anything down and never pay a fee until one has actually found accommodation and signed the contract. Estate agents are only entitled to payment by results (*Erfolgshonorar*) and not to expenses. Never sign anything you do not understand. If you do not understand the estate agent's contract, always show it to someone who does *before* signing it. If some kind of fee is required initially, go to another *Makler*. There is usually no shortage of them. Some are known to hand out lists of nonexistent accommodation or of accommodation which has already been let.

For a short-term let, nothing too much can go wrong, but there are still a few cardinal rules.

1 Never sign without understanding every word (small print and all).
2 Be clear about length of let or, if this is not decided in the short-term letting agreement, how long the period of notice is. This can be somewhat confusing, in that the let ends, for example, six

weeks before the next quarter after notice is given, which could mean several months' notice. In this case one can be liable to pay rent for a period after one has left!

3   Make quite sure you understand how the rent is made up. There are two different sorts of rental agreement:

(a)   *Inklusivmiete*: everything is included and not a Pfennig more is payable to the landlord (*Vermieter*) except for electricity, gas, telephone etc.;

(b)   *Kaltmiete*: basic rent for use of apartment or house; plus *Nebenkosten*: additional costs for heating, lift cleaning, stairwell, etc. These *Nebenkosten* usually add a third onto the basic cost, so it is essential to have those items constituting the *Nebenkosten* enumerated in or appended to the rent contract.

Some landlords unfortunately are not above calling the rent *inklusiv* and then adding on *Nebenkosten* afterwards. How can this happen? Very simply by not having a written contract, which should be insisted upon by the tenant if it is not provided already by the landlord.

One of the bones of contention between landlord and tenant is often the annual heating bill. If the rent is *inklusiv* (assuming central heating), it includes a monthly payment (*Pauschalzahlung*) towards the annual heating and hot-water bill, which is sent to the landlord by the administration (*Verwaltung*) elected by the flat owners in the block of flats concerned.

The amount of heat and hot water used by each tenant is computed by reference to meters (*Zähler*) attached to the radiators and the main hot-water pipe in the bathroom. These meters are read once or twice a year. They work on the principle of liquid evaporation measured on a scale. The warmth from the radiator evaporates the special liquid in a glass tube. This is not a very reliable method of measuring the heat used, but it is accepted as the best available. It helps not to have the meter covered by anything such as curtains or furniture or do anything which will accelerate evaporation. The hot-water meter consists of a dial which shows by a revolving arrow the quantity of water used.

If you are asked to pay a deposit returnable at the end of the lease, insist that it is placed in a savings account. You open a savings account at a bank and then hand the passbook to your landlord. In this way you earn interest on the money deposited. The interest will not be very much, but it all adds up. It also affords a pleasant introduction to a local bank, which you may need for other purposes. (See the chapter on Shopping and Money for opening a current account.)

If you do get into difficulties with your landlord, receive nasty letters and feel you are being treated badly, then the best thing to do is to consult the local *Mieterverein* (tenants' association). There is one in every town. It only costs a few Marks to join and you will receive every sympathy and, depending upon the quality of those who run the association, good legal advice.

Of course, if the landlord is someone whom you know well or has been recommended by friends, then many of the precautions mentioned above may prove unnecessary. But if the landlord is a stranger, it is worth being careful. It is a shame to find oneself landed with unnecessary extra expense.

**The caretaker**

The caretaker or janitor of a block of flats (*Hausmeister*, male, or *Hausmeisterin*, female) is someone to be taken seriously. A caretaker or even a *Bademeister* (there do not seem to be any *Bademeisterinnen*) in a public swimming bath, is a person with authority and he or she will not hesitate to use it regardless of the importance or sense of importance of the person being called to order.

If one lives in a block of flats, the *Hausmeister* is someone it is necessary to get on the right side of, if only because when something breaks down, he is usually the only person who can put it right, if (of course) he wants to. A *Hausmeisterin* does not usually repair things, but will usually take or pass on messages. The code of behaviour (*Hausordnung*) in blocks of flats, particularly in respect to noise (radio, television and using drills for odd jobs) should be taken seriously. Usually there are very strict regulations governing where not to park one's car and these should be observed in absolute detail. Using someone else's parking lot or garage space without their permission can make an enemy for life. If in doubt always ask. People will usually be most helpful if they see one is a foreigner, especially an English-speaking one. A few moments' consideration for others will pay enormous dividends in good will, especially with the elderly.

**Cleanliness and neatness**

One of the blessings of living in or visiting Germany is the cleanliness of the people and the place. Hygiene extends to smartness in dress and person. Germans are very clean and their clothes are usually immaculate. Apart from students, who soon resort to normal attire after leaving university, they find it difficult to look scruffy. They make allowances for foreigners, but they do not share the easy informality of dress of many British and American people.

A professor friend and colleague of mine, after being introduced to the Deputy Director of a British high-street bank one Sunday, said to me afterwards: 'A typical Englishman with creased trousers!'

The Germans are essentially an orderly people, not slavishly so, as is often suggested, but in practical ways. For example, the simplest German car has a hook for jackets, the more luxurious, a whole rail above the rear side windows. Everything they make seems to display an ability to think deeply about everyday conveniences. As a visitor, one comes to expect this sense of orderliness.

Germans are not only house-, but garden-proud. Even the smallest plot of garden in front of a modest-sized semi-detached house will have beautifully kept grass and an array of flowers and plants.

**Noise**

Even if you are not particularly sensitive to noise, please remember that others are and that noise is regulated by the *Hausordnung*. If you are, then it is worth paying attention to insulation and plumbing and also to the area and type of people who live there. If a blue-collar area, then it will be quiet during the day but noisy at night and over the weekend, when people are doing noisy little jobs at home or repairing their cars outside in the street. If it is a white-collar neighbourhood, there is a good chance that it will be quieter.

Noise in blocks of flats is always a problem. One night, after I had gone to bed, I heard blood-curdling screams from the flat above. I dashed upstairs and rang the bell. 'What do you want?' asked my obviously astonished neighbour. She was an elderly lady, totally unused to late-night callers. 'To rescue you,' I gasped. 'But I was only watching television!' she replied.

It is also worth seeing whether a new block of flats is going up nearby. Work on building sites begins punctually at 6 a.m. every weekday and can be very noisy.

### The plumbing

If you are sensitive to noise, check if the plumbing is noisy or not. This is not easy, because it is other people's noise that will disturb you. Yours will disturb others. I have lived in a flat where my bedroom was under my neighbour's bathroom. I heard every time she went to the loo.

I shall never forget one period of hearing the sound of an errant steam engine let loose in the house every morning shortly after 7 a.m. It was an excruciating chugging sound, rather like the scene in *The Lady Killers* where the old lady has to bang the kitchen pipe to stop the noise.

This particular early-morning disturbance went on for months without the caretaker being able to find out which of the tenants was unwittingly responsible. Finally there was peace for a few weeks in the summer. I mentioned this to the caretaker, who then said, 'Ah, it must be Frau Schulz because she is on holiday now.' When Frau Schulz returned, we pounced. When she turned on the tap the chugging sound immediately occurred; but she had not realized that she had been disturbing everyone in the house!

Ideally, though this presents problems, you should

ask your neighbours to do their ablutions while you are inspecting the flat. Obviously, it would make a strange impression to ring the bell and say, 'Good morning, my name is Smith. I am thinking of renting the flat next door and want to check the noise level of the plumbing. Please go and wash your hands.' However, I hate noise so much, I would do anything!

**Good insulation**

As it becomes very cold in a German winter, it is certainly as well to check the structure and the heating of accommodation offered. If it is a flat, one should ask when it was built. If before 1983, when the latest regulations came into force, there is the risk that the insulation is inadequate, which can lead to costly heating bills. It is not a bad idea to check the outside wall for proper insulation by tapping it. If made of concrete, it should have layers of insulating material. The window frames and double-glazed or special glass should also keep out the cold within specified limits. French windows out on to the balcony or garden should fit snugly, otherwise one is in for draughts.

If the method of heating is under-floor heating and the block of flats in question was built in concrete (*Beton*), then be careful too. My experience is that with the heating on in winter one has to keep opening the windows because the walls do not 'breathe' as they are not porous. When one open the windows for any length of time, the room becomes cold and the floor heating is unable to rewarm the room quickly. In other words, one has to keep opening and closing the window all through the night unless one wants to suffer a perpetual headache.

**Checking beforehand that everything works**

Apart from checking the plumbing for noise, one should in any case check that all the taps work, and especially whether the washers need renewing. Plumbers are extremely expensive, even for little jobs, because they charge for *Anfahrtszeit* (the time they take to reach you), and they are not always easily obtainable. If a tap does not function properly then turn on the control tap underneath or above. The tap should now work. Then turn it off to check whether it still continues to drip. If so, the washer is defective.

It goes without saying that one should check the lavatory to see whether the flushing system works. Landlords are always more willing to attend to such things *before* rather than after the lease is signed. The same holds for leaking radiators. The tell-tale sign is a white or greenish discoloration near the tap.

The carpet should be examined carefully for stains, dirt or cigarette burns. If the carpet is stained the landlord can have it cleaned, and if it has been burnt with cigarette butts, this should be noted down in the inventory. The same applies to every single defect as regards the fitments or furniture, particularly the parquet floor if there is one, so that you have proof that you are not responsible. And get the landlord or his agent to initial or sign it.

This is all fairly obvious, but it definitely pays to get things straight at the beginning rather than try and iron them out afterwards – usually at one's own expense because one cannot prove that one was not responsible oneself and one therefore loses a part or all of the deposit. The saving in time and annoyance will also be tremendous and well worth any embarrassment caused by being a stickler for detail.

## Children

One thing is very impressive in Germany: the provision of playgrounds (*Bolzplätze*) for children. Blocks of flats usually also have playgrounds for children and though they sometimes cause quite a racket, it does mean that children have proper facilities. (Sensibly, dog owners are forbidden to allow their pets to play in sand pits.) Flat administrators are, however, very strict about children not playing in or near garages, for obvious reasons of safety.

# Shopping and money

**Money**    German money is simple to understand and all too easy to spend. Notes are in values of 1000, 500, 100, 50, 20, 10 and 5 Marks (DM 5) and the silver-coloured coins are 10, 5, 2 and 1 Marks (the 10 Mark coin is usually only kept by numismatists); each Mark has 100 Pfennigs. There are 50, 10, 5, 2 and 1 Pfennig coins.

German currency has appreciated against every other since the end of the last war. This makes most visitors fairly price-conscious. One should remember to try to change one's coins into notes or simply use them up before returning home because home banks will not accept coins for exchange.

Money is not sacred in Germany, but it is of extreme importance. One does not leave small change about at home. If you do find a coin on the floor, spit on it for luck! That is the custom. Germans always keep loose change in a purse. This does have an advantage for men because trouser pockets do not develop holes frequently if kept free of change.

**Shopping**    Shopping in Germany is an art if one wants to get value for money. It is very easy to spend more money than necessary by shopping in rather too upmarket shops. Certain luxury goods can only be obtained in luxury shops, but often the same or approximately the same item can be bought cheaper in a more modest establishment or simply in a department store (*Kaufhaus* or *Warenhaus*), supermarket, hypermarket or cash-and-carry discount store.

There are some 300 hypermarkets, that is, stores with sales areas of more than 2500 square metres. They are becoming increasingly popular for the cheaper range of goods to the detriment of the larger stores, which are perforce trying hard to rationalize their strategies by reducing the variety of their goods and the number of suppliers as well as closing down unprofitable outlets.

It is worth shopping around for everyday necessities and groceries and of course one would not want to miss the excitement and bargain offers during the winter and summer sales (*Winterschlußverkauf* and *Sommerschlußverkauf*, respectively). Skis and other sports equipment and clothes may be bought with considerable saving. However, it should be remembered that goods purchased in sales are usually expressly excluded from exchange unless there proves to be a defect which was not mentioned or noticed at the time of purchase.

One should be careful in shops to ensure that the shop assistant fully understands what one wants *before* the purchase is completed and the transaction rung up in the cash register. Because of elaborate accounting procedures connected with a complicated tax system, no sales assistant likes cancelling a sale.

German stores are very security conscious. They bristle with television cameras and often have goods sensitized to detect light-fingered customers leaving with unpaid-for goods. They even have cameras in the loos to spot customers changing into stolen garments!

If one has cause for complaint against a shop or about the quality of goods sold or services provided, and it is impossible to get satisfaction from the person responsible, then one should consult the local *Verbraucher-Zentrale* (consumer association-cum-citizens' advice bureau). Though private, this is financed by the Federal Government and the government of the relevant *Land*. Whilst the *Verbraucher-Zentrale* has no teeth, it can offer advice and solutions to problems. Often knowing one's rights and quoting them will mellow the most recalcitrant tradesman or obdurate craftsman.

*Shoe repairs*

Shoe repairs are expensive and one can wait a long time before the repairs are ready. Shoe bars at stores are not cheap either but at least one does not have to waste time. Sometimes one may be lucky and hear of a good shoemaker who is reliable and not too expensive. Stick with him.

*Mail-order houses*  There are some 3000 mail-order houses in West Germany. If one is staying in Germany for a few months, it is well worth consulting the mail-order catalogues from such reputable firms as Quelle AG, Bauer and Neckermann Versand. These companies also have stores in the larger cities and agencies in the small towns and sometimes even villages. They are particularly good for electrical goods, especially if one has to invest in a refrigerator, washing machine, television or radio. The quality of mail-order goods is usually very high and the prices appreciably cheaper than equivalent products available in the shops. Often the two products appear and indeed are identical. Only the labels are different. Moreover the mail-order houses offer full service and repair facilities.

The only problem may be that when one returns home from Germany, it may not be possible to have electrical or mechanical equipment repaired or to claim under the guarantee.

*DIN*  When shopping for electrical goods it is a help to know that certain goods (electrical and mechanical) have to be tested for safety and carry a special label or ticket. Standards are drawn up and goods tested by the Deutsches Institut für Normung e.V. in Berlin (DIN for short). DIN standards are recognized the world over and cover most types of product: music cassettes, ball pens, light bulbs, batteries, bicycles, paint. It is a private organization financed by the dues of its members (companies large and small), revenue from publications and government grants.

*Getting a reduction*  A useful thing to remember is that when making expensive purchases Germans often buy *mit Prozent*, that is, they never pay the full price. Finding some way of getting the car, washing machine or television set cheaper than the list price may be normal for American, but is less so for British readers. One sometimes feels no German customer expects to pay or dealer to charge the list price. The discounts are officially for particular groups of people, such as teachers or members of a sports club or the like. However, a friend can often arrange a discount. Nevertheless, it is sometimes cheaper still to buy from a large store or supermarket. The only disadvantage is that one will have missed getting to know the friends or friends of friends who make buying with *Prozent* possible. Of course if one does buy cheaper through friends and the machine breaks down, then it is embarrassing taking it back for repair under the guarantee. One can only learn by experience.

There is never any harm in trying to reduce the price of anything, as long as it is not something official like a train or bus ticket! Even then, you will often hear the word *günstig* (reasonable) when someone is trying to explain how one can save time or money or do something more conveniently. The main thing is never to have any inhibitions about trying to get something cheaper. Germans are excellent bargainers and take a pride in it. Of one thing you can be assured. Even if you do get a reduction, the other will still have made a handsome profit on the deal!

**Souvenirs**

The best advice is not to buy in souvenir shops if you want to get value for money and obtain what is truly used and appreciated by the people of the country. It is far better to take time off from sightseeing to have a look round ordinary shops. You may find a useful household gadget; a jumper, jersey, shirt or scarf; porcelain (Germans do not use china) or glass; even chocolates. The municipal tourist advisory bureaux often have attractive publications in English, though not always very moderately priced. As in most countries, there is a lot of expensive kitsch on the market which is aimed specially at the tourist, though of course tastes vary and it is easy to be snobbish.

Before buying glassware or porcelain it is advisable to have a look round the appropriate sections of museums. Nymphenburger porcelain figurines are exquisite copies of the work of celebrated artists such as Franz Anton Bustelli. The same applies to porcelain from East Germany. Some Upper Franconian glass work is excellent.

One probably needs to take advice before buying paintings or drawings, but there are fine regional artists, such as the nineteenth-century Bavarian painter Carl Spitzweg, or the early twentieth-century painter Gabriele Münter, though works by these artists are expensive. (One can always buy prints.) It might pay to keep an eye open for local auctions. Christie's and Sotheby's have branches in Munich. There are many good modern art galleries in the main cities, especially Munich's Maximilianstraße. The annual *Dokumenta* exhibition at Kassel is also worth a visit. German antique silver, especially Augsburg, is very fine, expensive and scarcely obtainable. Nineteenth-century silver is interesting and affordable. Modern silver is often 80 per cent silver as opposed to the 92.5 per cent of sterling silver, and thus may not be classified as silver in the United Kingdom.

Other possible purchases that come to mind are candles, especially in preparation for Christmas, when the whole country seems alight with them: candles as table decorations in a restaurant or at home, a candle lighted when one is drinking wine, candles shining through windows, candles pictured gleaming from the covers of magazines, candles of intricate design and special candles made of beeswax – sweet-smelling to improve the air.

The angels sold at Christmas are colourful and attractive. They serve as excellent adornments to the Christmas tree or can simply stand on their own. Traditional and timeless in their appeal, they too sometimes carry candles.

Germany is also the home of children's toys. Middle-aged and senior readers might remember the clockwork Schuco cars made in Nuremberg. Now there are toys of greater sophistication shown at the annual toy fair there.

Finally one should not forget the wooded platters used by Germans for eating the traditional country meal of bread, cold meats and possibly radish or other salad vegetables.

There is nothing more fiendishly calculated to ruin **German** one's stay in a foreign country than confusion over **banks** money. You will probably be taking travellers' cheques and some cash in local currency with you. But there might be an occasion when you need money quickly from home. If you are going to be staying in one place for a few months, it is well worth establishing good relations with a local bank on arrival.

A good local bank is a very useful acquisition indeed. Get your bank manager at home to give you an introduction through the foreign branch of the bank's head office. In this way it should be possible to establish confidence quickly. Once this is done, you will probably be able to draw money in German currency on your home account by cashing British or American cheques. In other words, your own cheque becomes a traveller's cheque. Using a Eurocheque of course ensures this in any case, but only up to £70 per cheque. If you stay for a longish period, it is very useful to be able to use a cash dispenser.

Germans usually settle bills by credit transfer rather than by cheque. One hands in bills to the bank clerk, who then completes a money transfer order (*Überweisungsauftrag*) and debits one's account accordingly. This method is very convenient and saves postage. However, one should remember that there are bank charges, which are to some extent negotiable and vary from bank to bank.

One might prefer to deal with a savings bank (*Sparkasse*). Savings banks provide the usual services of cheque books, etc., and are a thriving form of banking in Germany. They usually belong to the municipality and are thus considered to be safer than ordinary banks. However, all banks now subscribe to an emergency fund which is used if a particular bank is in difficulty. Banks have collapsed in the recent past. In Germany there are more small private banks than in the United Kingdom, but in time they tend to get swallowed up by the larger joint-stock banks.

German banks are usually very helpful to visitors and seem to have an endless supply of local maps, calendars and diaries at their disposal. I have always found German bank personnel exceedingly kind and helpful. They are without doubt the nicest type of German, at this off-the-street level, with whom the average visitor will come into contact.

German banks offer an extensive range of services including, for example, those of an estate agent. They are often heavily engaged in the property market and are thus in an excellent position to advise customers in this respect. One should nevertheless consider very carefully before investing in property with their assistance by taking out a loan. However low the interest rates offered, borrowing money is always an expensive business (there are not only the money and interest, but also the not inconsiderable ancillary charges involved). It is a golden rule when doing business in Germany that the nicer people are, the more cautious one should be before signing any contract. Always get the other party to work out the full cost involved to the Pfennig and to initial the estimate as being correct in every way. Then go home and sleep on it. Never be embarrassed to ask questions, as many as are necessary until one has understood everything. And if things are not absolutely clear, ask someone else. Compare different banks. Never commit yourself until you are absolutely sure.

**Charges and fees**   Visitors from English-speaking countries may find it takes time getting used to the fact that the average German expects to have to pay for a number of services which elsewhere would be free. One is charged for the delivery of parcels; application forms for various permissions are charged for; certificates issued by government or local government officials are also often to be paid for; and at the railway station there are charges if one does not collect goods sent by express more or less immediately. The rationale behind levying these charges is to make the whole apparatus of government less onerous for the taxpayer. One does sometimes feel such charges are superfluous, for example when paying for the delivery of a parcel for which the sender has already paid postage (especially when the delivery of small packets is free). One just has to get used to a different way of doing things. The main thing is not to be unduly surprised and to realize that in Germany nothing or very little is free.

Service is usually included in hotel bills and one may or may not leave a few Marks for the room maid or cleaner. The better the quality of hotel and service, the more traditionally inclined one is to do this. Tipping taxi drivers is likewise optional. Porters charge fixed rates. For tipping in restaurants, see the chapter on Food and Drink.

**Tipping and services rendered**

In general, Germans in service are never insulted by receiving gratuities although they may protest out of courtesy. One does expect to pay and be paid for extra services. It is not unusual to help someone – give them a lift, help move something – and be offered a tip regardless of one's own social position. It is not meant as in any way demeaning, but simply as a thank you, to show that one does not take kindness for granted. This may seem more extraordinary to British than American visitors.

In Germany, and this is sometimes difficult for British people to get used to, people have no inhibitions about discussing money; and you should have none yourself. Nobody will regard it as vulgar or 'ungentlemanly'. Germans are too realistic for that. People assume that others need money to live.

Yet one should be clear of one thing. If one does expect to be paid for, say, writing an article or preparing a translation, then make this clear at the beginning. One should never assume that there has been a gentleman's agreement to remunerate one for extra trouble taken. The concept of a 'gentleman's agreement' is foreign to the German way of life.

# Living conditions and requirements

**The weather** Germans do not talk so much about the weather as the British are supposed to do. Often it is not to be talked about but endured: very cold in winter, down to −20° Celsius, and very hot in summer, up to 30° Celsius. Whilst German central heating takes care of the former, air conditioning is not so widespread as in the USA, and both Americans and British will find it very hot indeed. If you are going to tour by hired car in the summer, it might be worth trying to book a car with air conditioning, though this may not be easy to obtain. The saving grace in winter is that the sun shines so often, even on the coldest days, so at least it is cheerful however arctic it feels. There is generally a

*'I am from England, where the acid rain comes from.'*

welcome absence of the damp cold experienced in Britain, though parts of Germany share its muggy weather, particularly the south during the 'Föhn' wind (equivalent to the French mistral).

People complain that the Föhn affects their health and temper. Whether or not this is medically true, it is the case that there is an increase in heart attacks and circulatory problems during this period. If you do not feel fit, then you will know why. However, visitors may not notice the Föhn at all. In the Alpine foothills and in the mountains proper, the Föhn is the time to see much further into the distant landscape than usual.

Because everything starts so early in the morning in Germany, it is as well as a visitor to remember that meals are taken earlier – breakfast from seven o'clock onwards finishing usually at the latest at nine o'clock; lunch from noon (often for workers for only half an hour) and the evening meal from six o'clock in the evening onwards. In the winter some early risers and late workers lead mole-like existences. The main thing is that visitors for lengthy periods usually adopt different time rhythms to those at home.

**German time schedules**

Newspapers get delivered at unholy hours in the early morning. It is the practice to give the woman or young lad who does it a gratuity for Christmas. One can do this by leaving something at the central office of the newspaper concerned. Unfortunately, bread, milk and meat are not delivered to the door in Germany.

**Deliveries**

Most houses and blocks of flats have intercom with electrically operated door openers, so that when one rings one has to conduct a short conversation through a mini-loudspeaker outside. It takes a little getting used to. If you are a tenant, always be sure to lock the outside house door at night. Otherwise you will draw the wrath of other, security-conscious, tenants down upon you. Blocks of flats do not have porters to check visitors' credentials, as do some flats in the USA.

**Security**

Whilst you are much safer in Munich or even Frankfurt or Hamburg than, say, some parts of London or especially New York, it is none the less sensible to observe the usual security arrangements as regards locking outside doors and the rest, because if someone does happen to break in and one has not locked the outside door, then one is in some way morally if not actually responsible. This is very obvious, but its observance does prevent black looks from neighbours and ensures good neighbourliness for which, in an emergency, one is only too grateful.

*Beware of door-to-door salesmen* Beware of the smooth-tongued young salesmen or saleswomen who come to the door trying to sell magazine subscriptions, toothbrushes, matches, anything. Use the spy-hole, which most front doors have, to size up the caller. If you do open the door and the sales gabble starts, just say politely with a smile, 'Danke, kein Interesse,' and then smiling even more angelically, close the door. Don't, whatever you do, let such people into your flat or house, and even if you do that because you have a bull-mastiff to protect you, never sign anything. Once you do that you may need the help of an expensive lawyer.

Whatever you do, do not agree to pay some neighbour's bill without the neighbour having specifically asked you to do so. Tricksters come to your door and ask you to settle Frau Schulz's bill. The lady is not in and they, looking, oh! so honest, only come round once a fortnight to collect cash. It's all hooey. Most people settle bills by credit transfer and only the poor pay for newspaper subscriptions on the doorstep.

Finally, be extremely wary of the religious sects whose disciples are determined to save your soul over the weekend. *Don't let them in!* You will never get rid of them without wasting a great deal of time. If there is any trouble on the doorstep, say (this advice was given by a senior official with the local government), 'Der Herr Pfarrer sagt, Ihr seid vom Teufel!' (The vicar says you are sent by the Devil!), and then close the door looking demonic yourself!

In Germany keys are to be taken seriously. Keys **Keys (their** mean security, ownership and power. If one does not **importance)** have a key one is not part of the team, firm or whatever organization to which having a key entitles membership.

Everything is locked that does not need to be left open. As a visitor one imagines that Germans have a mania about keys and locking up offices, WCs, cupboards etc. After one has lived in the country for some time, one begins to appreciate the necessity of keys for preserving clean lavatories, general cleanliness and order. But it does take some getting used to.

If given a key, do not lose it. Have a special place for keeping it. The performance and cost of getting a replacement make it worth taking care of the original. Being given a key is a sign of trust, being withheld one of not being trusted or considered capable of looking after one. Keys are sometimes formidable in weight. You cannot take them lightly in more ways than one.

German garbage collection works extremely well. **Garbage** Everybody has to have a special type of dustbin or **collection** trash can which fits onto the garbage truck hoist mechanism. The dustbin is then lifted and its evil-smelling contents are deposited in the bowels of the lorry's grinding machine, which reduces the trash to manageable dimensions for disposal on municipal rubbish dumps. The process is extremely costly and flat tenants are charged more and more each year for this service.

Some areas have large containers set aside on the street for glass, others have separate containers for newpapers and cartons. Moreover the Red Cross and similar organizations collect paper and old clothes once a month. The municipality will usually collect old furniture and kitchen stoves and any bulky throwaways once a month. These collection days are announced and one often sees students and impecunious young couples selecting the odd item from heaps of discarded furniture. There are also the German version of rag-and-bone men who, for a fee (!), will come and collect your odds and ends. You pay for everything in Germany, even for disposing of the tyres you discard when buying new ones. You just get used to it.

**Laundry and dry-cleaning: hazards and joys!** Most flats are provided with washing machines or there are communal ones down in the basement. To use the latter you buy tokens from the caretaker. Otherwise you take bundles of dirty washing to the laundry (*Wäscherei*) which is usually combined with a dry-cleaner's (*Reinigung*). You will get your laundry back in a few days snow-white but with a slightly pulverized effect (I think they use molten lava and steam rollers!). As most Germans have their own washing machines or use communal ones in blocks of flats, there is virtually no launderette culture as in the UK.

If the dry-cleaner's for any reason loses a pair of trousers or reduces them to shorts' size, then you are in for complicated negotiations with the firm involved. Officially the dry-cleaner will accept liability up to 15 times the cost of the dry-cleaning. If you are not satisfied with such paltry compensation and want your rights, then you will need to go to arbitration. In this case you have to agree to share the cost involved with the dry-cleaner if the award does not go in your favour. If you are triumphant, you recover all, plus the compensation. Is it worth the excitement? Sometimes the dry-cleaner will try to solve the problem himself and often is successful. It is extraordinary how shrunk clothes can be restored to their pristine length.

If one is concerned about possible damage to an expensive garment through dry-cleaning, then one can insure it with the dry-cleaner for a few extra Marks. This is the advice of the consumer advice bureau (*Verbraucher-Zentrale*). Dry-cleaners should but often do not tell customers about this safeguard. Clothes seldom get lost. Every article accepted for laundering is numbered by the laundry on receipt. However, it is a good idea to complete the laundry list with due care and always keep the ticket.

Some of the nicest German ladies seem to work behind the counters of dry-cleaners, and it is well worth making friends with them. They have time on their hands, take a personal interest in their customers and know all the local scandal whilst preserving the utmost discretion in passing it on. In my experience, they also take pity on helpless bachelors, not only sewing shirt buttons on, but failing the appropriate button, actually removing one from another customer's beautifully laundered shirt with a wink and smile, saying, 'Oh, that doesn't matter, he's got a good wife!'

**Making a cuppa**

Kettles are not normally used in Germany. To boil water, one uses a saucepan on the electric hotplate or gas-stove ring. Or one uses an electric water-boiler, which is plugged into the wall like a toaster.

German teapots often do not have sieves so that if one uses tea leaves instead of tea bags, the leaves block up the spout.

**On the phone**

Using the phone in Germany takes a little getting used to. When ringing someone at home, it is usual to announce one's surname (or Christian name if intimate). 'Smith hier (here), guten Tag' or 'Grüß Gott' (depending upon whether in North or South Germany), and then 'Störe ich?' (Am I disturbing you?). The other person will usually say 'No, of course not,' even if you are, but will appreciate your courtesy. At the end of the conversation you say 'Auf Wiederhören' (Until next time), instead of 'Auf Wiedersehen' (Until the next meeting). Some South Germans repeat 'Grüß Gott' at the end of the conversation, and Austrians, when speaking to a lady, say 'Küß die Hand' or, very formal, 'Küß die Hand, gnädige Frau.'

When calling someone in the office the procedure is the same, except that one has to get past the switchboard and a secretary unless the person you want to speak to has a *Durchwahlnummer* (that is, a dial through number, or personal line). German executives and officials often have dial-through numbers, which make ringing from long distance much more economical. Telephoning in Germany seems expensive. One way to save money on calls if you do not know someone's dial-through number is to call the switchboard, ask for the number only and then dial the number direct yourself. You save the cost of being put on hold.

*Looking for a number* Looking up a number in a German telephone directory is an art if the institution or organization one wants to call is national or regional, e.g. Bayerisch*e* Staatsbibliothek (feminine, Bavarian State Library), Bayerisch*er* Rundfunk (masculine, Bavarian Radio), Bayerisch*es* Fernsehen (neuter, Bavarian Television). This is because German is an inflected language. So before you start to search for the organization, ask someone to tell you whether it is a 'der, die or das' word, i.e. whether it is masculine, feminine or neuter. You will save yourself a lot of time.

A further problem is that some institutions, especially government ones, are not given under the name of the organization itself and listed alphabetically, but under the name of the ministry responsible. Furthermore there are the vowels with umlauts, ä, ö, ü, which are abbreviations for ae, oe, ue, respectively yet follow names written in full. But in any case, the Federal Post Office is revising the procedure for the alphabetical ordering of names in the telephone book.

Names and telephone numbers of hotels are usually found in a section headed *Hotels*, rather than under the name of the hotel itself, unless it is very plush. The same holds for cafés and restaurants, which are usually grouped under *Gaststätten*. Most important of all, embassies are given under *Botschaften* and consulates under *Konsulate*.

A simple way out of any confusion is either to get someone to find the number for you, or to arm yourself with a local 'What's on?' or city guide in your hotel, which should list the most important addresses and phone numbers.

The saving grace in any case is that telephone operators usually speak enough English to cope. The fun can begin when dealing with Directory Enquiries to trace a number back home. The pub called 'The Windsor Castle' is often mistaken by European operators for the Royal Castle. If you get stuck, ask to be put through to the *Aufsicht* (the supervisor). Supervisors are super people and will take immense trouble to help. So just say, 'Die Aufsicht, bitte!', or more polished, 'Geben Sie mir bitte die Aufsicht!'

Like everything else in Germany, medical services are well organized, from the helicopter service which picks up people seriously injured in traffic accidents on the motorways, to the emergency service which operates in most urban areas for those urgently requiring a doctor or ambulance. The local newspaper publishes lists of doctors operating the emergency service over the weekend and hotels are obviously able to obtain medical assistance when required. British people are covered by an agreement with the National Health Service but need to show a certificate (obtained before leaving Britain from one's Department of Health and Social Security office). Those from further afield such as the USA will need private health insurance policies to take care of most eventualities.

**Emergencies – getting a doctor quickly**

There is a cardinal difference between how the medical services work in Germany and in the UK. Under the National Health Service a patient goes for non-emergency treatment in the first instance to a general practitioner who, if necessary, writes a letter of introduction to a specialist. In Germany the patient, usually without consulting his or her *Praktischen Arzt* (GP) goes straight to a *Facharzt* (specialist). The status of the *Praktischen Arzt* is not so high as that of the GP. If you have back trouble, go to an orthopaedist, or if you have eye trouble to an ophthalmic surgeon, do not bother the *Praktischen Arzt* unless you think it wise to take his or her advice first. All that will happen is that this doctor will pass you on to the relevant specialist.

The other point to note is that it is increasingly unusual for a doctor to visit patients at home. This task is usually reserved for the emergency doctor who, if it is very serious, will arrive in an ambulance, or by taxi if he is not attached to a hospital but is on the roster of emergency doctors on call. Doctors feel that home calls take a disproportionate amount of time and the fees they are allowed by the health insurance schemes to charge make them hardly worthwhile. In general, patients are expected to go to the doctor's surgery.

*Medicine from abroad*

If you have a health problem for which for one reason or another the appropriate medicine is not available locally and you need it to be sent out from Britain or the USA, then according to the law, the medicine will have in the first instance to be sent to a local chemist and not to you. It is therefore well worth stocking up with sufficient supplies before you leave home. Possibly it would do no harm to have a doctor's certificate translated into German, explaining the nature of your problem and the necessity of your having the medicine with you at all times. The unfortunate problem of drug addiction and the strict Federal control of medicines in use have necessitated greater stringency in the import of drugs.

**Coping with bureaucracy**

Germans have a different attitude to life from English-speaking people, which it is as well for the visitor to understand. The horrors and deprivations of the last war had a marked effect upon the older generation. Apart from this there is a general serious-ness about Germans, possibly a difficulty sometimes to take a relaxed view of life, which gives the visitor the impression that life in Germany is a very serious matter indeed. While visitors may not share this view of life, they might take it into consideration when trying to understand what is going on.

One cannot escape bureaucracy if one stays in Germany for any length of time. It pervades every aspect of daily life. If you stay for a year or two it becomes second nature. The phenomenon dates in Germany from Napoleon's day and the reforms he introduced. It has been there ever since and has managed to weather the storms of domestic revolu-tion and foreign wars until the present day. It shows no sign of abating and indeed seems to become stronger with every year that passes.

It is not an exaggeration to say that 'coping with *Little things* Germany' is to a great extent coping with detail – *count* tickets, identity cards, even rubber stamps. The big things look after themselves. This is because Germans tend to be masters of and take great pride in detail and in getting things exactly right. They have tremendous stamina for the minutiae of lists, certificates (*Scheine*) and the rest. This can be a wretched nuisance on the one hand but a blessing on the other: a nuisance when one has mislaid a particular piece of paper – identity card (*Ausweis*) or ticket which acts as an open sesame to some event or building; a blessing when one needs help to find a paper and immense care is taken. One gets exasperated and is then humbled by an unexpected bonus of the German way of doing things.

It is a mistake to try and swim against the tide. If a particular piece of paper is required, then make sure you have it, even if it all seems a waste of time. If there is a legitimate way round an obstacle, grasp it. But do not ignore a difficulty or requirement. And never appeal to an official to waive a regulation or requirement. Officials have no mercy; or mercy is really the wrong word, because a regulation is a regulation.

What an official might do is find another, more convenient, regulation which is usually the best way round an administrative difficulty. Supposing one wants to send something by a cheaper rate or import goods and pay less VAT. An obliging official will help find the cheaper rates. Or if permission is required to do something and according to one regulation this is not permissible, the obliging official may simply change the nature of the application so that another regulation applies, according to which the application may be approved. Often it is a game, but it does pay to learn the rules.

In Germany it always pays to read the rule book, to do research on any sort of permission which is required. By doing some background work on a subject you can show the official that you are being reasonable and he or she will then be delighted to help if he or she can. *Bluster does not help!* Threats to write to your MP, or the equivalent of *The Times* (the

*Frankfurter Allgemeine Zeitung* or in the south the
*Süddeutsche Zeitung*) will not help either, for the
simple reason that no one does, or if they do the
result is not the same. German ministers do not
immediately answer letters to the FAZ.

*Officialdom*   It is a fact of German life that most people (apart from
some young people) have a great outward respect for
what they call the State, in the sense that they as
individuals regard themselves as fairly powerless
against central control. This does not mean to say that
parents will not sue the local ministry of education.
They will and they often win, but this particular aerial
of the State is on a different wavelength. Officialdom
itself is not usually challenged, however much people
may complain against bureaucracy or what· they
sometimes call official arbitrariness.

The same holds in a German's relationship to the
police which, although it is improving, is still
strained.

The police are there to keep people in order. The
average policeman behaves perfectly correctly, but he
does not have the 'friendly bobby' image that the
British police have or used to have. The police are
treated with a certain reserve and this reserve goes
right up the social ladder. I have always found the
police most helpful, and there is no reason why
foreign visitors should not be treated in the same way.
No doubt much has to do with the significance in
Germany of a uniform. The man or woman in
uniform is sometimes very different to the same man
or woman out of uniform. Official rôles have a
greater significance than in English-speaking countries.

*Rubber*   Do not underestimate the power of the rubber stamp
*stamps*   (*Stempel* ). Often an official's or a business person's
signature on a document or at the bottom of a letter is
worthless without a rubber-stamp mark alongside.
Always insist that whoever gives you a document or a
receipt also stamps it. It is different if you are dealing
with a private person, but if he or she has a rubber

stamp, ask for a stamp mark on the document he or she has signed. It adds a further degree of validity to the document and the person concerned feels more committed than ever to honouring the agreement.

Business letters are often signed by two people, neither of whose signatures one can decipher. Savings Bank pass books have to be signed by two bank clerks and of course stamped when business is transacted.

Germans do take this sort of thing very seriously indeed and it is advisable for a visitor to do likewise to avoid all difficulty.

It is difficult for those from English-speaking countries to understand the power of government and the attendant bureaucracy which influence the average citizen's life to a far greater extent than at home. The general effect for a foreign visitor is more noticeable, the longer he stays. A prime example of this is the Post Office. Post offices are palaces of exactitude, where even the length and girth of letters are measured by post office clerks to ensure that envelopes conform to the prescribed measurements to avoid excess postage being charged.

**Coping with the Post Office**

It is particularly wise to avoid them during the rush-hour. However, if you really want to get the feel of Germany and understand the way of life, go into the post office, preferably in a large town. If you can cope there, you can cope with the whole country blindfold. You will see lots of different counters and possibly one with the word *Auskunft* (information) emblazoned across the top. Go there, explain your business to the official and he will tell you which counter (*Schalter*) to go to. If you go to the wrong counter, you have to start all over again!

Sometimes the Post Office comes to you. Understamped letters incur fines. The postman rings the bell – often early in the morning – and demands 66 Pfennigs. There is another postman who delivers parcels and he may levy another charge of DM 2.20 for delivering a parcel as opposed to a packet, for which there is no charge. Registered post has to be signed for by the addressee; if one is not at home a special journey to the post office is unavoidable, and there one has to prove one's identity. If one does not carry a passport or driving licence, yet another trip may be necessary. The same applies if the postman tries to deliver a parcel during one's absence. He leaves a chit saying that the parcel is available for collection at such and such a post office, which may be different from the post office where one collects registered mail. A way round these tedious difficulties is to complete a document enabling a friendly neighbour to accept post on one's behalf. The neighbour, who will then sign and pay the fees involved, can be reimbursed later. If these time-consuming details are not mastered, they can assume an importance out of all proportion to the time spent on them.

## Germany and the Law

One of the things that strikes one most when dealing with German officials at a senior level in any branch of government is that they are usually lawyers. As we have explained in regard to renting accommodation, it is the written contract and not the spoken assurance that counts. The expression a 'gentleman's word is his bond' has far less currency in Germany than it has – considerably watered down today – in Britain or other English-speaking countries.

This is not to say that Germans, as far as one can generalize, are legalistic, but that they attach far greater importance to unimpeachably clear verification; proof or evidence is needed. Contracts are required; and to interpret them lawyers.

It might help to explain some basic concepts of German law to make this clear. The constitution is a written one and was enacted in 1949. In it is enshrined a veritable Bill of Rights. The President of the Republic can refuse to sign a bill passed by both houses of Parliament (*Bundestag* and *Bundesrat*) if he thinks that the legislation is contrary to the Constitution. Law itself is divided between civil and criminal; the former is laid down in the Federal Law Code Book and the latter in the Criminal Code. Both are written down in paragraphs which are constantly being quoted, not only in court but in public too. For example, the attempt to legalize abortion became the Paragraph 218 Campaign.

As a visitor, it is unlikely that one will come into either conflict or contact with the law. However, the relationship between the average German citizen and the law provides an interesting insight into the way of life. Germans are not averse to going to law to obtain their rights from landlord, tenant, employer, garage, insurance company, local ministry of education or even from their neighbour. Going to court is not as prohibitively expensive as in some countries. Many people are in any case members of an insurance scheme which pays for most of the court costs and lawyers' fees involved. Furthermore, court procedure is not intimidating. Judges do not wear wigs, witnesses give evidence seated, ceremony is kept to a minimum and there is virtually no cross-examination of witnesses.

**Advice to exchange students**

Students planning their stay at a German university can save themselves considerable time and no little frustration by heeding the following tips.

1 First of all get confirmation of permission to study at the university (*Studienplatz*).
2 Take at least ten passport photos with you. You will need every one!
3 UK students should obtain the EI 11 form from the DHSS to ensure free medical services in Germany. American students, even if their insurance covers abroad, will none the less have to obtain medical insurance cover from the local state insurance office (the *Allgemeine Ortskrankenkasse – AOK* for short) before being allowed to matriculate at the university of their choice; and they will need to obtain a residence permit (*Aufenthaltsgenehmigung*), initially issued for three months, from the *Ordnungsamt*, which may be in the local guildhall or police station. American students should first arrange insurance with the *AOK* because, although they may be insured at home for a stay in Europe, German doctors insist on payment in cash unless

proof of local student, i.e. *AOK* insurance, can be produced. It is in any case obligatory for American students seeking to register at German universities and, compared to what the average citizen pays, a bargain at around DM 63 a month. And who knows? If you want to stay on, you are already in the system. Before the *AOK* will give insurance cover, one has to tell the official that one is being registered for entry to a university. American students are also required to obtain a clean bill of health certified by the local Medical Officer of Health at the *Gesundheitsamt* before matriculating. British students do not have to have an AIDS test to obtain a residence permit.

4 Both American and British students will have to furnish proof of financial resources either, as in the case of British students, with a certificate from the local authority which pays the grant, or with a letter from one's parents stating that they will pay all expenses incurred during the stay in Germany.

5 University libraries only lend books out to students who are registered with them and who are in possession of an identity card and a library number. Libraries usually close relatively early in the evening and are not open over the weekend.

6 It is advisable to try and obtain the University *Vorlesungsverzeichnis*, which is a book containing names of officials, lists of classes and lectures and a map of the university. The problem is that the university does not usually sell the *Vorlesungsver-zeichnis*; it can be obtained at a local bookshop, which requires payment in advance. Furthermore, as the lecture lists are usually drawn up six months before publication, they are not always very accurate; but at least the book does give the student an idea of what is going on.

7 It is worth noting that German office hours are usually 8–12 in the morning and not a minute earlier or later. When engaging with officialdom it pays to be early, so that one does not have to spread the whole procedure out over two days if one has omitted to bring a particular paper which has to be collected elsewhere and handed in to an

official. And don't forget that it is often not just the piece of paper or certificate you need, but the rubber stamp. Even if you have all the requisite documents and they lack the *Stempel*, you are snookered because 'the salt hath lost its savour.'

# German etiquette

**Manners**  Germans tend to have formal rather than easy manners. In North Germany daughters used to be taught to curtsey and sons to bow on greeting or being introduced to older people – people who are middle-aged now can remember this. The south has always been less formal, although even now one does tend to bow slightly to the other person either if he or she is more senior or one finds oneself in a more formal situation.

German manners are in many ways different to manners elsewhere. Although on public occasions Germans possess tremendous patience in listening to lectures and speeches, German students have no inhibitions about whispering or even talking to their neighbour during a lecture. If it is impossible to find a neighbour to talk to and the lecture is excruciatingly boring, one just reads a newspaper or simply gets up and leaves. That is not bad manners, but academic freedom. Students will also turn up late to lectures and seminars and find nothing strange or even discourteous in so doing.

Moreover it is not always the case that if someone bangs into you by mistake, he or she will say 'Entschuldigen Sie bitte' (Excuse me please), 'Verzeihen Sie' (Forgive me, Pardon). He or she may say nothing or even simply squeeze past you in a queue or crowd of people without saying a word. Bavarians sometimes just say jocularly 'Hoppla!' (Whoops!). Such behaviour may seem rude to English-speaking visitors, but it is certainly *not* meant to be.

In this case it is a question of a different use of language. Certain courtesies are intended but not expressed in words, especially when asking other people to do things, such as fill in forms or perform services. Requests to a waitress for a cup of coffee, or by a policeman for an identity card, can sound rather curt, if only because of the customary use of the imperative. It is important to remember that people in situations like this are not being rude, but straightforward. The many expressions of politeness in English sound equally strange to the German ear.

Germans – and this can be chastening – expect the British to behave like ladies and gentlemen. They have the saying 'Das ist nicht die feine englische Art' (That is not the courteous English way of doing things). They, Germans, have been taught in school that all English people are friendly and polite. They still believe this.

Germans do not claim to behave any other way than naturally. To say of someone, however respected in public life, that he or she behaves naturally is the greatest compliment one can pay that person. Good manners really consist of simple natural behaviour, though it does get overladen with the ritual of greetings.

**Greetings and 'wish-greetings'**

As a general greeting at any time of day one says 'Grüß Gott!' (good day) in the south and 'Guten Tag' in the north. One can say 'Guten Morgen' (good morning) but only 'Grüß Gott' or 'Guten Tag' in the afternoon and then later 'Guten Abend' (good evening) and later still 'Gute Nacht' (good night). Added to these standard greetings is a large collection of, for want of a better term, 'wish-greetings'.

Supposing someone calls to take you out to dinner. The person with whom you are staying and who is not accompanying you will say to those going out to dinner, 'Viel Spaß noch' (Have fun) or, if you are going to the theatre, 'Viel Spaß im Theater'; or if someone calls in the evening, at the end of the conversation he or she might say: 'Schönen Abend noch' (Hope you have a pleasant evening). Some people will wish you luck or a pleasant time if they know that you are going to do something like go shopping or go for a walk. Or on saying 'Good night' to someone who is driving home, one would add, 'Kommen Sie gut nach Hause' (Get home safely), or to someone going on a journey, 'Gute Fahrt!' (Have a good journey) or on holiday, 'Schönen Urlaub' (Have a nice time); or after a chat, 'Mach's gut' (Good luck).

Teachers beginning a term at school will wish one another a successful start to the term. There are many variations of the wish-greeting. They hold for the many public holidays, not just Christmas and Easter as in English-speaking countries, but also for Whitsun or even the weekend. It is always polite to use these wish-greetings, although the depth of sincerity is mainly pro forma. One notices if people forget them.

Then of course there is the wish-greeting before beginning a meal, 'Guten Appetit' (roughly the same as in American English, 'Enjoy your meal'), though in German high society one tends not to say it. In some families, everybody joins hands round the table and chants 'Guten Appetit, guten Appetit'.

One of the especially nice things about these ritual wishes is that it is regarded as impolite to enter a place, say a restaurant, without greeting the people there – 'Guten Abend' – and on leaving saying 'Auf Wiedersehen' (good-bye) or in the south 'Wiederschaun'. It takes very little to learn the wish-greetings and yet is most rewarding as a short-hand way of being accepted linguistically by German friends and neighbours.

**The German home**

German homes differ from many British ones, though not necessarily American ones, in their generally being labour saving, efficiently heated and always spick and span. They tend to lack the lived-in appearance of many British homes. In flats there is often a dining alcove instead of a dining room to save space. The focus of the living room is the table in the middle, around which easy chairs are arranged. It is usually around the table that visitors are invited to sit in the evening and drink the inevitable glass of wine or *Schnaps* (liqueur), or in the afternoon to drink coffee.

Furniture tends to be either modern or reproduction Biedermeier or English. Sometimes the eye will light on a nice old piece – a cupboard or chair – which escaped the war, but mostly Germans have had to buy new furniture because they or their parents were bombed out. Those with aristocratic names, with the prefixed title *von*, may have photographs of their family's former country house or castle framed nostalgically on the wall. Interesting but sad.

**Visiting**

Germans are eminently house-proud. Although often both husband and wife go out to work, their homes are always embarrassingly spick and span. Always wipe your feet demonstratively on the doormat before entering the house or flat even though your hostess will tell you not to bother.

Take some flowers (*Blumen*) unwrapped. (This involves juggling in the car or at the front door to hide the florist's wrapping paper without getting transfixed by the pins which hold it together!) Or take some chocolates (*Pralinen*). Your hostess will always tell you that you shouldn't have bothered and how naughty you are, but it is definitely the custom. Some small gift from home, say tea, is greatly appreciated. Tea and coffee are exceedingly expensive in Germany. But don't take a hostess red roses the first time she and her husband invite you! All parties might get the wrong idea.

I remember attending a party once, arriving punctually and watching the other guests arrive. They had all brought the traditional bunch of flowers and they all seemed to have bought them from the same florist. The flowers were identical. The bell rang, the hostess opened the door, greetings, hand-over of flowers; 'Oh how kind of you, but you shouldn't have bothered' from the hostess, who then ushered in the guest and disappeared with the flowers into the kitchen where presumably there was an inexhaustible supply of vases! It was a ritual. I always wondered what happened at the end of the day when the hostess was confronted by a dozen identical bunches of flowers!

One of the trickiest things is timing. If you are invited to a supper or dinner, be punctual because your host or hostess may have timed what is cooking with utmost precision. Germans do not appreciate late guests. If they say 7 or 7.30 they mean it, not 7.30

or 8. The great problem is when to leave. 11 p.m. is usually too early, unless of course your hostess and host obviously look tired. If everybody is enjoying themselves, and you will usually sense this, it could be a very late evening indeed. If your host or hostess is a VIP or has a very demanding job, then an early departure, unless you are really and explicitly pressed to stay, will be appreciated. If they yawn then go; but do not interpret this as a gentle hint – they are genuinely tired. Likewise, when you have guests for dinner at your house, expect them to stay possibly to all hours, and take it as a compliment and not as a sign of boorishness if they do.

If you invite students for a glass of sherry before supper, be assured that if they enjoy themselves you are going to have to share your supper with them. So it is better to have a buffet with the sherry or wine. Germans are very warm and honest in this respect. It is the custom of the country.

Sherry is drunk as an aperitif, but wine rather than sherry parties are held. There are no cocktail parties as such. The Anglo-American habit of drinking on one's feet and circulating with a word of small-talk here and there is not the custom, although Germans do stand at large parties. They tend to sit and drink wine or beer with their guests at a table, as they do in pubs as well; one does not usually stand or sit at the bar in a German pub. People like to have a corner or alcove fitted in rustic style rather like a pub and drink there, or sit round a table in the middle of the living room.

**Table manners** German table manners are different from English ones. One does not put one's hands or hand in one's lap whilst eating but on the table. Knife and fork are held differently and often suspended in the air while munching. Fish is not cut but gently prised open with a knife or the flesh separated from the bones with a dessert spoon; likewise potatoes.

Table water is not usually drunk. Alcohol (beer or wine) often is. One raises one's glass and says 'Prost' or 'Prosit' (informal) or 'Zum Wohl' (Your health, more formal). The formal rituals of passing the port round to the left and ladies leaving the table after dinner are virtually unknown in Germany. If your health is drunk, you drink it as well! That is the custom. If someone offers a toast to you at dinner, it is discourteous not to drink your own health.

If you are invited to someone's home for an informal evening meal, then ten-to-one it will be to *Abendbrot*, a cold supper consisting of sausage, cold meats with pickles and either tea (often with the choice of rum in it, which tastes delicious) or beer. One also eats lots of bread with the meal, and those who are not used to it should go slow on the bread because it does tend to make one's stomach feel alarmingly full. The same warning holds for the celebrated dumpling (*Knödel*) – eaten at lunch or supper – of which there is a large variety in South Germany varying from the very substantial Bavarian type, which is eaten with hot fat or gravy poured over the top, to the lighter, fluffier Bohemian kind. Whichever type you eat, do not underestimate its ability to fill you up. *Knödel* are so appetizing to eat, but once inside the over-indulgent eater can give one the feeling of having swallowed cannon balls!

**Signing the guest book**

The Germans, being on the whole a very literate people, will often ask first-time visitors to sign the family guest book. So be prepared if after coffee and cakes or dinner, a guest book is produced. A brief glance at it will reveal that a number of previous guests have been journalists or on occasion minor poets. This may make you feel only semi-literate as you shamefacedly merely pen your name when your hosts so obviously expect a dedication or a ditty. But do not worry. Just sign your name and be gone! Here are a couple of useful phrases to keep up your sleeve, quite literally:

Vielen Dank für eine wunderschöne Zeit.   (Thank you very much for a lovely time.)
Vielen Dank für einen wunderschönen Abend. (Thank you very much for a lovely evening.)

I admit that I just sign the book and slink away,

though on one occasion when I had really enjoyed myself staying the night in a medieval castle, I wrote that I had had such a truly wonderful time, I hoped I would be invited again. I never was! So the best advice is just to sign, leave and put your all into an eloquent letter of thanks.

**Formal thanks** When writing to thank one's hostess for hospitality or simply when writing to a married woman, one uses her Christian name as opposed to her husband's: Frau Helga Schmidt and not Frau Heinz Schmidt. Replying to formal invitations is usually done by phone and, if in writing, seldom in the third person singular. The formal British custom of writing to thank one's hostess for dinner is also not always practised. Everything is far less formal.

**Cards** It is not the custom to send everyone cards at Christmas to the extent one does in English-speaking countries. Relatively few Easter cards are sent. However there are occasions when one tends to rely more upon the printed word, i.e. a card rather than a personal letter to inform one's friends and acquaintances of an engagement, marriage or death.

**The overcoat ritual** There is etiquette involved in helping people on with their coats. When you visit an official he usually insists on taking your coat and putting it in his wardrobe cupboard. Every official seems to have one, the more senior the official, the larger and more impressive-looking the cupboard, which also holds less official-looking things like bottles of lemonade. At the end of the interview the procedure is reversed. The official retrieves your coat from his cupboard and offers to help you on with it. If you are fairly young, you thank profusely, but protest against so much concern and quickly put the coat on yourself. If you are much older than the official and do not mind admitting it, then you let him help you on with it. The whole effect is rather spoilt if your coat is a very shabby one or just an anorak! To refuse the offer of help, you should say, 'Danke, aber ich bin noch nicht zu alt' (Thank you, but I'm not as old as all that). But if you are old, just let him get on with the job. There is a joke where someone excuses himself being helped on with his coat by saying, 'No thanks, that's how I lost my wallet the last time!'

Germans (apart from young lovers) do not usually kiss in public except at the railway station after a long journey. Possibly this is changing now; opinions among young Germans on this subject vary. Children do not always kiss their parents before going to bed, either. Germans demonstrate their affection and respect in a different way.

**Kissing and shaking hands**

Shaking hands is a ritual on its own. It is usual to shake hands on meeting someone and at the end of the ensuing conversation before moving on. It is regarded as a great insult to refuse to shake hands with someone. So when in doubt shake hands! There is little or no social distinction involved. One shakes hands with a porter or a cleaner if the occasion arises. Germans are very democratic in this respect.

Only civil marriages are officially recognized. Many couples have a church wedding afterwards. It is no good going dewy-eyed to a local priest. He cannot officially marry you, though some young people imagine he can.

**Marriage and death**

Should you decide to marry a German, do consult your consulate well in advance if you want to get married in Germany. You may well find that the necessary paperwork is so daunting that it might be simpler, however absurd this sounds, to take your loved one back home and get married there. German bureaucracy is formidable at any time but when it comes to getting married, all sorts of certificates are required. Unless it is a true emergency (birth of a child or one of the partners is at the point of death), there will not be any wedding without all the paperwork. Once all the certificates are present and the local registry office ceremony has taken place, do check all the documents which are handed over to you. You may find that your name and other important information have been spelt wrongly.

The engagement ring is worn on the left hand then

converted to a wedding ring and worn on the right hand. The same ring is used for both functions.

Dying is simpler, but exceedingly expensive. It is not a very pleasant eventuality to have to think about, but in Germany one thing is clear. If the relatives of the deceased are not quick, the body will be buried locally. Health regulations in this respect are very strict indeed. Both burial in Germany and transporting the body home are very expensive and the paperwork involved considerable. One should inquire about relevant insurance or settle for cremation, but even the latter, though cheaper than the other alternatives, is assuredly more expensive in Germany than at home. Whilst this is not a very cheerful subject, it can be made all the more unpleasant by not being prepared.

**Funerals**   It may be that one is invited to a funeral. Black or dark clothes are worn. At a large official funeral, one signs one's name in a book and then usually receives a card thanking one for attending. If the deceased is not cremated and was well-known in life, there will usually be a funeral address at the graveside.

Afterwards, as in English-speaking countries, one condoles with the relatives and will be invited to the *Leichenschmaus* (refreshments and drink). The first toast is always to the departed, and thoughts include the living. In villages the custom is to try and drown one's sorrows. The American-style funeral parlour does not exist in Germany and most funerals seem to be arranged by the municipal authorities, who also own the cemetery. It is a very expensive business for the deceased's estate or relatives.

# Business etiquette and ethos

When making a deal, it is the contract which counts, the written word and *not* the oral assurance. Contracts usually state 'Nebenrede Zählt nicht' (verbal assurances are not legally binding). Contracts have to be in accordance with the law. It pays to know the law in order to evaluate the contract.

There is not really a code of behaviour based on so-called gentlemanly behaviour. The nearest one can get to this would be correct behaviour. The term *korrekt* has a certain moral connotation. But to say somebody's action was incorrect means very little. Eyebrows will be raised, but little else.

Remembering that it is the law and not any social or moral scale of values which counts, caution and openness are essential so that one's German business partner knows exactly what you want and mean. One has to go into great detail, take notes, be absolutely certain that one has understood what has been said and that the other person knows this. Leave nothing vague or unclear. Great stamina and perseverance may be required. But once all the possibly tedious variables have been dealt with and everything is as watertight as it can be, then one can be assured that from the German side everything humanly possible will work. All technical specifications will be kept to, the tolerances never exceeded.

The preliminary work involved will be repaid many times over. But your German partner will expect the same from you. Let him down on a delivery date or quality control and you are out. It will be done very politely and with all respect for your feelings, but you are quite definitely out. No excuses are acceptable or, if they are, very seldom. Some British exports have unfortunately performed woefully in the past, in terms of poor quality,

**Efficiency**

unreliable delivery dates etc., giving rise in Germany to the term 'the English disease'. If you establish a reputation for reliability, then you will have the most rewarding business relationship imaginable. In Germany it is achievement (*Leistung*) which counts, nothing else.

**Business hours** 'An early bird catches the worm' is a saying most apposite of German enterprise. Whilst it is possible to go for a peaceful walk at 7 a.m. in the morning in Britain, it is impossible in any German town. 9 a.m. feels like mid-morning. Most people are off to work by 7 and many shops open at 8 a.m., bakers' and shops selling milk earlier. The bonus of starting early is that one goes home earlier. If one wants to do business in Germany, one needs to be or become an early bird too.

One usually has breakfast at 7 a.m., and building workers and the like who start at 6 a.m. usually have their second breakfast at 8 or 8.30 a.m. Everybody lunches from 12 noon, Between 12 and 1 p.m., office workers lunch and a skeleton staff are on duty. Some organizations close between 12 and 2 p.m. For office staff and factory workers the lunch hour is officially 30 minutes only, and in factories the only other break is the breakfast break.

**Entertaining clients** Business is very much an intrinsic part of German life but yet quite separate from private life. Germans have no equivalent of the gentlemen's club, where business is never overtly discussed but people of like persuasion and profession belong. Therefore socializing during business deals cannot be conducted at clubs. Germans entertain mainly in hotels or restaurants and sometimes at home, but they sometimes find it a strain to bridge the gap between business and social relationships. These are cross-cultural differences which should be taken into consideration by English-speaking businessmen visiting Germany.

One thing is important. If you are a sales representative visiting the country and hoping to sell to a local firm, then it is you, the visitor, who is expected to invite the German customer out to lunch or dinner, and not the other way round. The fact that you are a visitor to the country makes no difference. Some visiting salesmen seem unaware of this custom, which unnecessarily irritates potential German customers.

Following two world wars and the end of the **Status** monarchy, with the attendant downfall of the old aristocratic order, Germans have become very democratic. One is careful to be discreet about visible signs of status at work. At universities there are no faculty clubs, as in the USA, or senior common rooms, as in the UK; similarly in factories and large firms there is one canteen for management and workers. There is a car park for all, though there may be (but not necessarily) parking lots for the chairman, deputy chairman and other senior staff.

The general idea is that each member of an organization is shown respect. Everybody is addressed with *Frau* (Mrs) or *Herr* (Mr), be he the managing director or the cleaner. People are very rarely addressed solely by their surname or Christian name, unless it is by their mates. The managing director will be addressed as *Herr* (or *Frau*) *Generaldirektor*. The more formal the relationship, the more likely one is to address a senior person by title rather than name.

The whole question of status and how it is shown is a complicated one. It is implicit rather than explicit. People know their place without the visuals to emphasize the point. The boss will address the cleaner as Herr Schmidt, and the latter the former as Herr Generaldirektor; but both know their place, though they may eat in the same canteen, even on occasion at the same table, and share the same car park.

Appearances can deceive the observer. I am certain that in the minds of the individuals concerned the difference in rank is more firmly registered than in the UK or USA. The reason for this seems to be that in Germany academic qualifications count for more in business. Herr Schmidt probably attended elementary school, which he left at 16 or 17; his boss may well have gone to a *Gymnasium* (grammar school) and university, and hold a doctorate too. Herr Schmidt knows that his boss is better qualified

Unemployment is still embarrassingly high in Germany. Herr Schmidt in this situation is pleased to have a job.

**Strict divisions**

People in very senior positions – say the Präsident of a university – would never think of inviting junior members of staff to supper or dinner at home. A professor would not normally invite his assistants home to supper either unless he wanted something extra out of them. There is the story of an assistant who presumed to send his professor a card at Christmas. When they met afterwards, the professor said: 'Lassen Sie das!', in other words, 'Don't do it again!' One does not mix business with pleasure.

Of course there are office parties at Christmas, on birthdays and the like. Indeed the courtesies involved in bidding farewell to employees entering on retirement or leaving to start a family are punctiliously observed. There is usually a company annual excursion, but many people find an excuse not to take part, and prefer to work instead. Business and free-time activities are completely separate.

**Industrial relations**

Trade unions play their part in Germany's prosperity. They may complain. They may mastermind the occasional crippling strike, but the last thing they are going to do is to try and cripple the whole economy. Industrial relations in Germany are based on the spirit of compromise. There is a worryingly high rate of unemployment, but in general it is a prosperous economy and society, especially for the workers with their own houses, televisions, cars and holidays abroad. No one wants to endanger this. German trade unions are not enemies of capitalism. Another point is that some German unions have been up to their necks in tricky legal battles with the authorities about illicit financial dealings, which have shed a rather lurid light on union leadership.

**Professionalism and education**

The high esteem in which academic qualifications are held in Germany was mentioned earlier. Seldom do people stumble into professions; they have to be fully qualified, at least on paper. Importance is attached to qualifications for all kinds of jobs; and the system of apprenticeships still flourishes, producing a constant stream of skilled workers. German business people tend to be well educated, both generally and in their own field of business.

The educational system in Germany is itself geared to this professionalism. Whereas British schools legally act *in loco parentis*, responsible for the physical and moral well-being of their charges and therefore attaching importance not only to academic work, but to team games, moral education, etc., schooling in Germany is seen more as a system of streaming people into different professions and grades of employment. It is left to the parents to bring up their children in other respects. Education represents a meal ticket for the future. Thus parents will pressurize teachers to get their children into the *Gymnasium*, which they hope will guarantee a plum job later. Parents will take teachers to court for allegedly unfair poor marks.

The traditional British system of educating an élite for the good jobs (in public schools and the old grammar schools) used to inculcate certain norms of behaviour, an unwritten social code which made possible such understandings as the gentlemen's agreement. Such a uniform code has never existed in Germany, and to this absence one is tempted to attribute the importance of the written contractual obligation. There is certainly in Germany no self-perpetuating élite resulting from the old-boy network of élite schools (although it is true that, as elsewhere, the children attending the selective schools in Germany often come from the professional classes). German society is as mobile as it can be, based on individual achievement.

Education is further discussed in the chapter on German Society.

# Problems of communication

**Friendliness**  Friendliness and helpfulness to foreign visitors can vary according to the situation and the region where one is staying. Obviously people will usually help visitors find the way, answer requests for other information etc., but beyond that Germans may appear impassive, reserved and not especially welcoming or forthcoming to the visitor. They tend to remain very private people in public.

There is sometimes a grey zone of reserve and possibly a lack of self-confidence. It is difficult to define. After having lived in Germany for many years and seen the sort of lives people live and how hard they work, one can understand that for many Germans, life is a very serious, all-absorbing business, which allows for little relaxation or time for others outside one's own immediate circle.

I have no statistics to prove this. My observations are purely personal, yet my English-speaking friends confirm this. As far as I can observe Germans do not seem to have the same at-one feeling or attitude towards each other which, even if it is at a superficial level, Australians, Americans and British people have. German society does not seem to have the same cohesive quality. No doubt the aftermath of the war, the fact that many Germans are refugees from other parts now under foreign rule, and other causes of social upheaval go a long way to explain why this should be so.

There is another interesting aspect of this lack of cohesion in German society. There is not the same tradition of unpaid service to the community as one finds, for example, in Britain. There are of course many people who give themselves tirelessly to the service of their fellow men, but communal service has not established itself as a tradition. It is the State which is supposed to look after problems which in some other countries are the concern of charities and other private institutions. The private initiatives in ecology and other areas tend to be politically oriented rather than devoted to specific problems.

Most Germans speak some English, some very well. **Language** Nevertheless, it helps to arm oneself with a few key expressions. Effective use of language shows that vocabulary is more important than impeccable grammar, knowing the single word and being able to pronounce it recognizably to the native ear is the best way of getting a specific thing or service. Pointing to it and sign language as to quantity help too.

Be patient if the locals seem to be slow on the uptake. Often one has got the right word, but the wrong pronunciation. The German 'o' is pronounced differently to the English: 'tot' (dead) more like 'taut' and not like 'not'. Often too an English speaker will emphasize the wrong syllable: 'Hánover' instead of 'Hanóver' in German. Often it is these simple yet fundamental errors which frustrate communication.

Germans do not share the same cultural traditions with English people which enable one to chat with ease. It is sometimes jolly hard work to keep the conversation going, but if one can find out what the other is a specialist in, then it is rewarding just listening and putting in the odd question to keep the flow of explanation going. Listening is often the best form of communication when one is a visitor to a country and is not fully conversant with the language.

A great difference between the two languages is in written etiquette. Letters to officials and business letters are written in a formal language and impersonal style. An application to an official is really addressed to the institution he represents rather than to the person himself. The tone is cool, the language rather wooden and no attempt should be made to be amusing or convey one's personality. Basically it is one machine writing to another.

This written formality underlines the distinction between the two words for 'you': the formal *Sie* (used for either singular or plural) and the informal, intimate *Du* (thou, singular). Never ever confuse the two either in writing or in conversation.

*Sie and Du*  Germans can always remember your name and take a pride in doing so. To forget someone's name is regarded as a sign of getting old or somehow past it. Names, that is surnames, have a greater significance than in England. *Sie* is more impersonal than *you*. By using a person's name you establish a special relationship with him. But never use the first or Christian name as in the English-speaking world, because this means using the familiar *Du* (thou) form which is usually only reserved for friends and relations. The exception here is young people, especially students, who often use the informal *Du* form even if they do not know each other. Sportsmen do the same. Colleagues at the office are usually *Sie*, that is *Frau* or *Herr X*. All women over a certain age, regardless of marital status, are referred to as *Frau*.

The *Sie–Du* question explains some other inexplicables to the English-speaking mind. For example, the fact that people having a drink in a pub together or a meal in a restaurant usually go Dutch. The English system of paying for rounds is seldom practised. Germans are not embarrassed by going Dutch, and the waitress usually asks at the end of the evening or of the meal 'Zahlen Sie getrennt?' (Are you paying separately?). It is a mistake to try and force a German to accept your settling his bill unless he is your guest. Treating someone implies a sense of obligation, reciprocity. People like to be independent.

This often applies to female guests. Women will often insist on going Dutch in order not to incur a sense of obligation, though normally, as a foreigner, if one invites a lady to a meal, she will accept the host paying the bill without a sense of obligation.

The younger generation is more matey than the old, but *Sie* is still generally preferred because the collegial relationship is usually kept distinct from friendship. Work and pleasure are kept separate. The intimate *Du*-relationship, which involves a high degree of trust and warmth, has a far greater significance than the American or British easy first-time Christian-name rapport.

When people decide to enter the *Du*-relationship with one another, they drink *Brüderschaft* (brotherhood), that is, each hooks the right arm in the partner's so that one can drink to the other. Then one shakes hands and is *per Du* with the other person. It does not always happen this way, but it is the traditional and undoubtedly the nicest way of crossing the threshold of friendship from *Sie* to *Du*.

The trouble is that the foreign visitor will of necessity usually only experience the formal *Sie*-relationship and merely observe the *Du* informal one from a distance. The difficulty is then to reconcile the two in one's mind to understand what is really going on. One also has to interpret gestures, smiles and verbal expressions.

German is a complicated language for English-speaking people to learn because it is, like English used to be, an inflected language. It is therefore for the learner a language rich in subtlety. In everyday usage, however, it is simple and without embellishment, and without the many courtesies of English that Germans find unnecessary. People tend to use the imperative mood more than one would do in English. A bank clerk may say 'Sie müssen hier unterschreiben' (You have to (must) sign here) and not 'Würden Sie bitte hier unterschreiben?' (Would you please sign here?). At best he will say 'Unterschreiben Sie bitte' (Sign here please). Although the imperative is used it is *not* meant as a command. The word *müssen* (must) is very much part of the language and keeps cropping up in situations where it would not do so in English.

A typical example that might lead to misunderstanding: 'How do I get to the station?' you might ask someone. The answer would be 'Gehen Sie geradeaus, dann müssen Sie sich links halten. . . ' (Go straight ahead, then keep going left. . . ). There's none of the English 'Well you keep going on straight ahead and then keep going left.' Germans use *müssen* (must)

*Sources of misunder-standing*

without meaning it imperatively, although to the English ear it might sound so.

Resist the temptation to translate literally from English. 'Are you warm enough?' (an innocent enough question in English) becomes highly insulting as 'Sind Sie warm genug?' because the sentence means in German 'Are you randy enough?' Or if you have the services of a German secretary or typist, be careful how you translate 'Let's open a file.' If you say 'Machen wir einen Akt' instead of 'Machen wir eine Akte auf' (i.e. using the word *Akt* instead of *Akte*, that is the masculine instead of the feminine form of the word, and omitting the preposition *auf*) one has said 'Let's go to bed', or even worse!

*Bad language*   One often hears the word *Scheiße* (shit) but few other swear words are used. One hears in Bavarian *Kruzifix*!; but one can listen to young people speak without every word being a four-letter one. Perhaps this is connected with the fact that although there are of course thugs and one reads about them in magazines, one is not really overtly aware of them.

**Gestures**   What Germans fail to express in words they do most eloquently in gestures. We have already mentioned the importance of shaking hands. There is one particular gesture for money which is made by rubbing the left thumb over the inside surface at the top of the second and third fingers of the same hand. The sexual gesture is made by sticking the thumb between the second and third finger whilst the fist is clenched. Another interesting gesture is plucking or pulling the lower eye-lid, which means 'Watch out!' or 'I don't believe you.'

Sometimes on the motorway you may see one driver make the so-called *Vogelzeichen* (that is, tap his forehead with his index finger) to another to express his displeasure, probably because the other will not let him past on the fast lane. Whatever the reason, the gesture is regarded as an insult, indicating that the person referred to is crazy or stupid. To give the *Vogelzeichen* is punishable and offenders can be fined or even imprisoned up to a year (though the latter happens very seldom).

Gestures can sometimes cloak meaning rather than reveal it. There is nothing devilish in smiling in a seemingly friendly fashion and saying something that in English would not usually be accompanied by a smile. There is nothing false either. It is a polish which English-speaking people do not expect and it is very easy to misinterpret, to take the smile at face value. It is sometimes important to realize that Germans for historical reasons have often been forced to temporize. They have rarely enjoyed the democratic freedom to speak their minds. This is not to say that on occasion a German will not speak his or her mind and it can be quite uncomplimentary; but in negotiations, for example, one has to be able to separate outward expression from true meaning.

If one has apparent grounds for complaint, how does one go about obtaining satisfaction? First of all, is it worth the trouble involved? Remember that there may be a language barrier which simply resulted in misunderstanding in the first place, and may make matters still worse. Sometimes it is cleverer to do nothing, just learn from the experience and avoid repetition.

**How to complain**

If, however, one feels aggrieved, then it is essential first to find someone who speaks English and understands yours. This may not be the person who originally dealt with the matter. Try to find the person in charge or as near to the top as you can go. Whoever it is, explain the problem as coolly as the circumstances allow and express the opinion, if this does not sound too absurd, that you are sure whoever was responsible only made a mistake and did not offend on purpose.

The great thing when dealing with Germans is not to shout (as some visitors do so regrettably) but to be as charming as possible so that they do not lose face, in particular the culprit. Remember, if the problem is a surly hotel clerk or rude waitress, and you can get what you want without the other losing face, you are assured of proper attention next time. Otherwise there may be a recurrence of whatever went wrong before, but this time it may be done in such a way that redress is well-nigh impossible.

If the person does not lose face, he or she may do you a favour to make up for the previous misunderstanding. If this happens, do not forget to mention it to the person to whom you reported the matter in the first place. It all oils the wheels and helps other visitors, as well as facilitating international understanding. It *will* be appreciated.

The culprit who was rude or unhelpful may have been only acting on orders from above. It may have been the fault of the manager who so kindly put the matter right. Often there are wheels within wheels in such matters. Once Germans know what you want, you will, within reason, usually get it. Nobody wants a fuss or a complaint (*Beschwerde*). Loss of temper (however understandable) will not help, even if you notice (and one can frequently) that the average German's temper is fairly short. But that is how they may behave to each other, and even in losing one's temper with someone in public, there are rules to be obeyed. It is better not to try it on as a visitor, but this is obvious enough. If all else fails, the local *Verkehrsamt* (tourist information office) will usually sort things out. Usually everything works out.

**Humour and the risks involved**

Beware! Germans appreciate some but not all British and American humour. Be careful of jokey idioms. 'Keep still! Or have you got ants in your pants?' could be understood literally! Teasing is dangerous because it may also be understood literally. 'Come on. Hurry up. Isn't the tea/coffee ready yet?', meant as a joke, may be understood as serious chiding. Don't risk being a wag until you know someone well enough and even then, still be careful!

Traditionally, German humour is often more subtle and cerebral than funny ha-ha. There are many learned German books on humour, especially irony, but one often suspects the authors would be too serious to laugh at the jokes lesser mortals make. Life is often rather a serious business in Germany and what English-speaking people regard as a joke might

*'Don't be silly – you know they've got no sense of humour.'*

be mistaken for flippancy by a German. He or she will make allowances for foreigners, but it is as well to be cautious so as not to give offence, which is of course the essence of courtesy.

Once on the right wavelength, an audience geared to Anglo-Saxon humour will enjoy laughing and be most appreciative. Germans do have a sense of humour, but it is different. Once a German realizes you are trying to offer light relief, he or she will respond quickly. Somehow you have to indicate initially that you are not being serious.

One place where you will easily get Germans laughing is in the pub at the so-called *Stammtisch*, the table where the regulars congregate. Having downed a few litres of a potent brew, one's listeners are ready to laugh. It is essential to realize that in Germany there is a time and place for everything. A joker is not appreciated in the boardroom. Nevertheless, if one does in a very tense situation manage to break the ice with a joke, the rewards are surprisingly great.

Germans are sometimes delighted to relax their official roles and show their gratitude by being accommodating. But one has to be careful. Beginning a lecture or a talk with a joke is fine, but care should be taken to choose one that the audience understands. There is nothing worse than just one person laughing. Too many jokes mean that one will not be taken seriously. A happy medium is essential. Rugby humour and dirty jokes are not necessarily appreciated, however crude some cartoons and photography in the local press may appear.

**Subjects to keep off**    There are certain subjects which should not be broached unless the person one is talking to obviously wants to talk about them. The war and Adolf are taboo unless, as so often happens, one's German colleague or host mentions both himself. This happens especially among the middle-aged or older generation. When you get to know a German, it is almost unavoidable.

Some Germans are compulsive talkers on the subject. They need a foreign audience because their own people are so fed up with the subject and want to forget it. However it is always interesting, especially eye-witness accounts of what it was like to live under dictatorship. The most interesting, yet possibly most harrowing, accounts are those of the Russian campaign. Whoever managed to come back alive is usually either a very lucky or resourceful person. One learns much about the Russians too.

What the last war has done for German patriotism is decisive; love for the fatherland really only extends to rooting for German soccer teams and tennis idols. The older generation is still patriotic, but certainly not the younger. People have become wary of patriotism, distrustful of military might and are imbued with fervent desire for peace.

Patriotism itself is at a discount. Indicative of this is the fact that Prussia, as a separate political entity, no longer exists, however present it may still be in older people's minds and loyalties. Vast stretches of territory which used to be German are now no longer so, though many refugees from former parts of Germany now Russian, Czech or Polish, or simply from East Germany, dream of a united Germany. Furthermore a German's loyalty, especially a South German's, is essentially to his region: a Rhinelander's to the Rhineland, a Swabian's to Swabia and a Bavarian's to Bavaria. Because West Germany is a federal state, the rights of the individual *Länder* in education, justice, environment and health are jealously guarded.

Speech, that is accent, is no indicator of class in Germany. An aristocrat from the south does not necessarily speak High German and most probably has the accent and to some extent speaks the dialect of the district where he lives. The more educated a person, the more selective he may be in the use of vocabulary and grammatical structures, but the accent usually remains regional. Southerners claim that their German pronounciation is true oral German and that German as spoken in the north approximates to the written language only.

**Accent**

Aristocratic titles are officially part of the name: Graf Landsberg; but they no longer denote (or are officially supposed to denote) aristocracy. Graf Landsberg will sign a business or official letter 'Graf Landsberg'. *Baron* is a tricky title, because it is only used in South Germany. It is, so to speak, a courtesy title for *Freiherr von*.

**Aristocratic titles**

The important distinction to note is that when addressing a titled person, one does not preface the title with *Frau* or *Herr*. Frau or Herr Baron Landsberg would only be said by a shop assistant, employee or servant. The same holds when writing to a titled person. It is no doubt unlikely that one will meet socially a senior member of the aristocracy. In any case such exalted personages usually speak English, so it is not necessary to torture oneself with all the German linguistic niceties. It used to be the custom to address royalty in the third person plural: 'Majestät haben geruht mich kommen zu lassen' (Your Majesty sent for me). Nowadays one addresses such people as *Sie* as one does the man in the street. Some people still use the title, more out of respect than conviction: *Hoheit* for Highness; but are then careful to continue with *Sie*.

Title holders are in general only accorded respect

when the title is accompanied by money and land.
There are many aristocrats from Silesia (now belonging to Poland), the Baltic States (now part of the
USSR) or even from East Germany who have lost all
their possessions. Titles have really become anachro-
nistic. Resentment is still felt against the late Kaiser
and his court, and the same holds for the former royal
House of Hohenzollern. This is not the case for all
aristocracy, indeed in some country districts, landed
aristocracy is treated with great respect and regarded
with no little affection. Some of the former regional
reigning houses, such as the unmilitary Wittelsbachs
in Bavaria are still revered. But the passing of the
German aristocracy has not generally been mourned.
The warm welcome given the Queen of England does
not mean that Germans yearn for the return of the
monarchy. Quite the reverse. Monarchy, Empire and
militarism tend to be regarded as an unholy trinity of
disaster.

**Academic and professional titles**

Academic and professional titles have supplanted the
social ones. *Herr Professor, Herr Doktor* or *Herr
Dippplom-Ingenieur* – on paper, visiting cards etc. –
tend to mean more than *Baron* or *Graf*. *Herr
Generaldirektor* or *Herr Präsident*, say of university,
mean even more. An academic without a doctorate is
regarded, in the words of one professor, as being
'naked'!

A *Herr* or *Frau Doktor* (not medical) is a person of
distinction. The title even graces a make of pudding,
sauce and muesli (Dr Oetker). When streets are
named after someone, the doctorate is included:
Dr-Würzburger-Straße. A former Munich clothes-
hire firm was called *Dr Schmidts Kleiderverleih*.

Although it is an offence to call yourself a 'Herr
Doktor' when you are not one, people do. Moreover
shop assistants will address customers as 'Frau' or
'Herr Doktor' as a sign of respect regardless of
whether the person has or has not got a doctorate.
Sometimes too – this used to be very much the
fashion and is still especially true in Austria – the wife
or widow of a 'Herr Professor' or a 'Herr Doktor'

would be referred to as 'Frau Professor' or 'Frau Doctor', regardless of her true academic standing.

The German word *Meister* (master craftsman) also has a different significance to the English word 'foreman'. The foreman in a British garage, for example, would in Germany be a *Meister*, but to become a *Meister*, one has to take a special exam which is set by the relevant guild or craftsman's organization. In every form of craftsmanship only a *Meister* may be entrusted with the training of apprenticeships, be it a cook, automobile mechanic or hairdresser.

*The Meister*

There is no monarch, but there are many monarchical elements in the social structure, be it in government, party or business. The average German works for or belongs to an organization which has someone at the top: the *Chef*, e.g. Franz Josef Strauß in Bavaria, the late Dr Karl-Heinz Beckurts at Siemens, or the President of a university. Someone is always at the top, and his colleagues identify themselves with him, and their subordinates with them, right down the ladder. There is an unwritten code of loyalty and respect. Chains of command are rigidly adhered to. Respect for the chain of command is expected from subordinates. The term *Chef* has something mystic about it. Possibly it is a reminder of the semi-feudal relationship which used to hold between ruler and subject until the end of the nineteenth century and even beyond. Undoubtedly, Germans strive to be democratic (there is worker participation in business and industry), but they think very hierarchically. They are not graded socially, but academically and professionally instead.

*The Chef*

What makes 'coping with Germany' easier is the ability to get through to individuals. Although the *Sie*-relationship is one of reserve sometimes bordering – for English-speaking people – on unfriendliness, it is not meant in that way. Suspicion and disillusion with strangers, are, in a sense, simply built into the German way of doing things, as a result of the war

**The people**

and so on. Such behaviour is *not* meant personally, because the personal relationship is expressly excluded.

The same person who may be off-hand on the street could be extremely helpful if he or she knew you. It is a problem of establishing trust and confidence. The British, for example have a background of reassuring social indicators based on speech (accent), education and family background. There is a history of internal peace and tradition, which Germans lack. They have grown up to be dis- and mistrustful.

However, once one gets through to a German, he or she will be as helpful as one could wish. It is a question of crossing a particular threshold. It could be at traffic lights. You are in the wrong traffic lane and want to get into the right one. Wind down the window and speak to the driver alongside. Could you possibly drive in front of him to enter the right lane? Usually he will agree and let you through. Try and drive in front of him without asking and you make an enemy for life. It is really getting to know people that counts, breaking through the barriers in a personal way. This often requires considerable patience, but it is something which brings great rewards in practical and human terms.

It is as well to remember that Germans often seem to live and work under great stress. In showing people kindness and an awareness of them as human individuals, it is not too fanciful to think that you are repaying them in some way for past afflictions. English-speaking people have historically often been on the winning side, Germans often on the losing side. This is not the place to delve into philosophy; but a certain knowledge of German history does give one an understanding of how Germans think and act.

**How to make friends**

Getting to know Germans varies. At the superficial level, acquaintanceships are often quickly struck up in pubs. One has to be the convivial pub type to make the best of this sort of situation. In general, people tend to be reserved in cafés. Camping friendships seem to blossom and last. No doubt the close proximity of campers sharing the same facilities helps. In large cities there is usually an Anglo-German Society (*Deutsch-Englische Gesellschaft*), where one can be assured of meeting interesting or not always especially interesting people. For younger people such clubs sometimes have a young people's group, which meets in a pub and arranges hikes, excursions and other activities for young people.

The reserved, less gregarious visitor will find it more difficult to get to know people. Hobbies or special interests often lead to meeting people of like persuasion – in visits to, for example, libraries and museums. Churches provide the opportunity for meeting people of similar views. One can usually join in social occasions organized by the parish. Culture is revered in Germany, and first-class concerts, theatrical productions and films are to be found all over the country. Some people even find the sauna a good place for getting into conversation with others. Or, of course, one can wait for carnival time. Not knowing the language is a disadvantage, but remember that many Germans, especially educated ones, speak English reasonably well.

In connection with social life in general, it is interesting to see how some Germans do look for a partner, by advertising for a spouse in the newspaper. *Die Zeit*, the *Frankfurter Allgemeine Zeitung* and other national newspapers include such advertisements. Of course the small papers do so as well, but the interesting thing is that people from all walks of life choose their partners this way. The FAZ publishes a booklet to help people word their advertisements effectively. They publish on an average 100 *Ehewunsch Anzeigen* every week and before Christmas, Easter and Whitsun the number increases dramatically. No statistics of success are kept but the paper receives a succession of engagement and wedding cards. One woman even found a husband for her orphan goddaughter this way.

One wonders why this form of getting to know someone is so popular, and whether it is a way of

*Advertising for a partner*

escaping one's own environment and breaking through the *Sie-Du* threshold into the unknown.

People use the same method simply to get to know others, not necessarily for marriage but for other relationships as well.

In local papers prostitutes, male and female, also advertise their services, although some papers refuse to accept advertisements from homosexuals.

# East Germany

It is worth including a chapter on the German Democratic Republic because the fate and history of that country are so entwined with those of the Federal Republic. However, one chapter is obviously not exhaustive, and only those things which one can do whilst being based in West Germany are emphasized, such as visiting East Berlin or the Leipzig Fair. One could and should write another volume on East Germany because it is so different to West Germany in so many respects.

One does not visit East Germany for the kind of holiday spent relaxing in luxury. The régime certainly comes as a shock to many a Westerner, and if one is anywhere near the Wall, its barbed wire, guards and dogs are an inescapable reminder of the less pleasant aspects of the East German system. But there is a great distinction to be made between some régime diehards and people as individuals! – even individual functionaries – who can be most kind and helpful.

I remember, for example, awaiting a vital letter from Munich while working in a library in Potsdam. The letter took an age to arrive and I went to the post office many times to enquire its possible whereabouts. Presumably my post was being examined by an official somewhere. Eventually I said to the post office official, 'I know that you will not confirm that somebody is holding up my mail, and that even if you knew who it was, you would not tell me. But perhaps you could ask that person to make an exception and speed things up.' He was very nice about it and the result was initially not that I received the letter I was waiting for, but that all my post from the UK arrived by special delivery. Ultimately I did get the letter from Munich. People at the library told me – after they had warned me not to complain – that if I had not been so insistent I would still be waiting. The point of this story is to emphasize the kindness of the postal official rather than to criticize the régime.

The interesting contradiction was that I had been drilled by friends and relations to keep off politics. To my astonishment, I found the last thing the East Germans wanted – members of the Party included – was for me to keep quiet. People were delighted when I discussed politics and seemed enthralled that I was an avowed monarchist.

Obviously one should be careful, and be absolutely certain that whoever one is with really does want to discuss things. One does not want to embarrass people or even make difficulties for them by forcing one's own views upon them. But if individuals on ordinary, informal occasions want to talk, one can

*'You don't seriously expect them to buy your old flared jeans?'*

feel free to do so. East Germans are very interested in what is going on over the Wall. Now they are officially allowed to watch Western television. But even before they were permitted to do so, many did.

To make a sweeping generalization, the East Germans may appear more friendly than West Germans. Their humanity is, in a sense, less obscured by a competitive lifestyle. In some respect the East Germans are more conservative than the West Germans; one should never go and sit down in an East German restaurant without being shown to one's place, and guests wearing washed-out jeans are simply not allowed in. Tipping is allowed and welcome.

The German Democratic Republic is a treasure trove of cultural history and the arts. East Berlin, the capital of the GDR, has showcase tourist facilities as well as its cultural jewels. These include the statues of Alexander von Humboldt and Frederick the Great, the Pergamon Altar in the celebrated Pergamon Museum, the Museum of German History, the thirteenth-century Marienkirche (Church of St Mary) and the Berlin cathedral, which is being rebuilt after its demolition during the war.

**What to visit**

Bertholt Brecht's house can be visited, as well as the famous Alexanderplatz, which has been an inspiration to many writers. There are many theatres and concerts too, together with variety shows and cabaret. The GDR Government tended to look askance at reminders of Prussian history, but has now invested considerable sums of money in restoring severely damaged and sadly neglected buildings, such as the Opera House.

One of the most interesting excursions is to visit nearby Potsdam, the former royal garrison city. Here one can see Frederick the Great's celebrated palace of Sanssouci and Cecilienhof Castle, where the Potsdam Agreement was signed in 1945. Sadly the historic *Garnisonskirche* (a mere torso following war damage) was blown up by the authorities, no doubt as a symbolic gesture of breaking with the past.

Of course, one cannot do justice in a few pages to

what there is to see, and this is not intended as a guidebook. However, the obvious places to visit outside Berlin and Potsdam are Leipzig, famous for its industrial fairs; Dresden with its historic architecture and celebrated art gallery (Die Zwinger), its museums, the Hofkirche (the court church) and the porcelain factory (for the famous Dresden china); and Weimar, the thousand-year-old city which became an important centre of German Classical literature and philosophy in the eighteenth and nineteenth centuries. Goethe, Schiller, Wieland and Herder among others made the town renowned. Nearby on Eltersberg Hill stands the National Buchenwald Memorial, situated on the site of the former concentration camp where 56,000 people died. The camp at Ravensbruck can also be visited.

**Television**  It is very interesting to watch East German television, affording as it does the opportunity to see an Eastern-bloc country in action – the meetings of solemn-looking delegates listening to long speeches, visitors from other communist countries or leaders of communist-sponsored groups in the West. Moreover, East German television shows Russian and Polish films, dubbed in German, and some excellent British oldies.

**Entry formalities**  Foreign visitors to East Germany need a visa. They can either obtain it at the GDR embassy in their own country or they can apply there for permission to receive a visa (*Berechtigungsschein*) so that they can obtain the visa at the border. Motorists can also book hotel accommodation at Interhotels through Berolina, the GDR tourist agency (the address is given at the end of the book). Those visiting the GDR (not transit) and not staying at Interhotels are required to exchange a daily minimum sum equal to 25 East Marks.

Visitors to West Berlin may visit East Berlin daily between 7 a.m. and midnight. The visa is obtained at the border and costs DM 5. Foreigners may only cross at Checkpoint Charlie (at Kochstrasse in the West, Zimmerstrasse in the East) or, if travelling on the subway, at Friedrichstrasse station, which is already in East Berlin.

One does need to take certain basic precautions. **Precautions** Avoid photographing anything which could possibly be mistaken for a military or railway installation and do not take any Western reading material, particularly newspapers (except the *Morning Star*) with you. Do not wrap up shoes in old newspapers, which could be read. Have nothing on you which could be construed as Western propaganda material. This is particularly important at border crossings.

This advice may seem exaggerated, but simple things can cause considerable annoyance. There is the story of the man who had grown a beard since his passport photo was taken and found himself in difficulty at the border in consequence. That problem was easy to solve (he merely had to shave), but what if it had been the other way round?

There is nothing to worry about if you are in a group and do nothing out of the ordinary. If you are travelling by car you are on your own and should be careful to observe all the regulations.

A particular word of warning is needed about the currency situation. Whilst living standards have improved immensely since the war, East Germans still suffer shortages of accommodation, materials, goods and services. Hard foreign currency is what most people want, because with it one can buy Western goods in the Intershops (shops primarily for tourists, selling luxury goods for hard currency). Although the official rate of exchange is one West German Mark for one East German, the black-market rate is one to fifteen or more. However, great discretion is required. Exchanging money on the black market is illegal, and the offence is treated very seriously. In a sense it is unfair of Westerners to exploit the situation, if only because at the official rate of exchange one can still get value for money. However, the requirement for visitors to exchange a set amount of money a day at the official rate can be rather inconvenient. Diners' Club and American Express cards are acceptd at state-controlled international hotels, stores and service areas. Travellers' Cheques can only be changed into GDR Marks.

It is important to remember that the import and export of GDR Marks is not allowed. Any other currency brought into the country must be entered on the requisite currency certificate and produced again before leaving with GDR gifts and purchases. Otherwise a licence is required for which a fee is charged.

**Travel**   One way to try East Germany out is to visit the Leipzig Trade Fair or take a weekend break to East Berlin. Berolina (the GDR tourist agency in London) offers a number of tours. Intourist, the East German travel agency in the GDR, also has special offers to East Berlin and to other parts of the country, and it is worthwhile to compare these offers with those of Western travel agents who include a visit to the GDR as part of their programme. An especially interesting Intourist trip is to follow in the footsteps of Bach or Haydn.

*Driving in the*   To quote from an official leaflet: 'The consumption
*GDR*   of alcohol or narcotics before or while driving is strictly forbidden.' This should be taken seriously. So should speed limits: 62 mph on the motorways, 49 mph outside built-up areas and 31 mph in built-up areas. The police can be very severe. They can levy hefty fines on the spot or forbid one to drive further. They are particularly hard on West Germans – but they have always been very helpful to me.

Road tolls are payable on the motorways for private cars and motor coaches with up to eight seats, including the driver (for distances of up to 200 km, 5 East Marks; up to 300 km, 15 East Marks; up to 400 km, 20 East Marks; and up to 500 km, 25 East Marks). In rural areas the only petrol one can use – and even this is not a very high octane – is obtainable at service stations on the motorway, and this may be some distance from where one is staying. It is as well in any case to consult one's garage about changing the timing to cope with the lower grade of petrol.

Although there is a breakdown service, it is as well to take a fan belt and other spares with one because the East Germans may not have the right type or size. Or, if they do have replacements, such as Halogen H 4 bulbs, they could cost three times what they would cost in the Federal Republic. Recently an agreement has been signed betweeen East and West whereby motorists in transit on the motorway will be afforded emergency assistance comparable to that provided by the West German Automobile Club (*ADAC*) in the Federal Republic.

Cycling is not encouraged for tourists. To quote the *Cycling* official leaflet again: 'There are no border crossing points (for cyclists) . . . The opportunities for hiring bicycles are very limited.' Recently restrictions have been lifted to the extent that motorists and rail passengers may take their bikes with them.

Driving conditions to Berlin have improved. Not **Driving to** only has the East German stretch of motorway from **Berlin** Hanover (the E 30) been repaired (with financial help from the Federal Repbulic) but other sections, such as from Jena to Weimar on the E 40, have also been attended to.

There are four routes to Berlin: from Hamburg (frontier crossing Gudow/Zarretin), 220 km, taking approximately three hours; from Hanover (frontier crossing Helmstedt/Marienborn), 168 km, taking approximately two hours; from Frankfurt (frontier crossing Herleshausen/Wartha), 344 km, taking approximately four hours; and from Nuremberg and Munich (frontier crossing Rudolphstein/Hirschberg), 270 km, taking approximately three and half hours.

The direction to West Berlin is well signposted, but one should not confuse West Berlin with the sign to 'Berlin Hauptstadt der DDR' (Berlin capital of the GDR), because the routes diverge. One should not worry if one goes past a turning-off point because there is a *Wendekreis* (a special turning point).

There can be delays at the frontier, but foreign visitors in transit usually have no difficulty as long as they obey the rules; that is, have the necessary papers (passport and log book as well as a Green Card for insurance), keep to the motorway (one can be fined for deviating from it), do not exceed the speed limit and do not take too long. Border officials become suspicious if visitors in transit take too long on the motorway. The officials check the time of arrival in the GDR with the time of exit.

If one has taken an 'unreasonably' long time, and does not have convincing a explanation, they assume one has met up with an East German or done something nefarious en route, such as distribute Western literature inimical to the East German Government. If the border guards or police suspect anything they will conduct a time-consuming search of car and passengers.

In spite of all this, there is usually time for drivers in transit to stop for a meal at a services area where, at the Intershop, cigarettes and drink are sold cheaper than in West Germany. Payment must be made in hard currency and not in East German Marks, which one has to exchange at the rate of one West German Mark to one East German. But please remember it is forbidden to drive after having had a drink. Moreover, smoking is forbidden during the lunch hour in the restaurant.

# German society

This chapter looks at a few key aspects of German society: education, the media and two characters of German life, the *Kleinbürger* and the *Beamter*. The loose link is that all are aspects of German culture; and as the German concept of culture is interesting in its own rights, it too is worth a brief discussion.

The concept of *Kultur* is broader, deeper and more nebulous than that expressed by the English word 'culture'. It is not only connected with the arts and education, but has overtones of spiritual and national values which are taken very seriously, despite reaction against anything connected with the Nazi years, when the word summed up the whole idea of Aryan Superiority.

**Kultur**

*Kultur* is expressive of the German penchant for abstract thought and theorizing; and also of the generally well ordered way the Germans have of doing things, of taking great pains and going into detail. It is no accident that German scholarship has excelled in the two most theoretical of academic disciplines, philosophy and theoretical physics (although it could also be argued that lesser scholarly minds strive for profundity at the expense of clarity).

At a more prosaic level, the breadth of the term is clear from a few examples: the regional ministries of education used to be called *Kultusministerien; Esskultur* means the aesthetics of fine food; and *Wohnkultur* means quality of life in a house or flat, in terms of both interior decoration and one's own lifestyle.

Perhaps one can say that Germans have a profoundly sensitive approach to everyday things. Nothing is done in a slapdash way; people take pride in doing everything the right way.

**Education**     Children are beautiful, cheeky and normal in every way, a delight to observe and – what appeals to the visitor – absolutely natural and unsophisticated. German children appear completely free. Indeed in many respects they seem, as in America, to rule the roost. However, free as children undoubtedly are, the minute school starts with the picturesque custom of going the first day carrying a large cornet of sweets, the serious side of life begins with a vengeance.

The trouble with German education is that too many people are too highly qualified for the jobs available. 3924 teachers in Bavaria alone and 27,400 in the whole of the Federal Republic are unemployed. Even doctors are unemployed, and those who are able to open practices are forgoing the custom of writing a thesis and thus becoming officially 'Herr Doktor' in order to reduce the period of training and start earning a living. Accordingly those with higher qualifications are making do with less well qualified posts and those with few or no qualifications are making do with no job at all. Pupils leaving secondary modern schools without the final exam are finding it increasingly difficult to obtain employment.

Progress in school decides a child's future job and social position. Parents are so well aware of this, and some are so ambitious for their children to achieve often more than they have managed themselves, that they subject their children and themselves to great – sometimes unnatural – pressures. Often parents not only insist that their children do their homework, but do it for them too.

Here is where success and tragedy occur, especially at the end of the school year when the reports are ready. These contain grades which indicate a child's future progress – whether he or she will make it to *Gymnasium* (the selective school where children can take *Abitur*, which gives them the constitutional right to enter university) or to *Realschule* (intermediary school where children take the *Mittlere Reife*. Whereas *Realschule* provides the future bank clerks and junior executives, *Gymnasium* educates those who will go to university and later occupy top positions in commerce, industry, the civil service and politics.

Tragedy occurs when children are forced beyond their ability. Municipalities have set up advice centres for anxious parents and distraught children. There are also emergency telephone lines for children in distress about their marks. Suicides are not unknown.

The situation varies from school to school, from class to class and from family to family, but it is the case that all is not well, as the number of court cases between aggrieved parents and ministries of education on the one hand and the sometimes very tricky problem of maintaining discipline in the classroom on the other shows. The latter problem is sometimes acute in urban schools, especially in the *Hauptschule*, the school which caters for the least gifted pupils. A distressingly large percentage of these leave school without passing their final exam. This reduces their chances of obtaining a job on the already contracted labour market even more.

The encouraging aspect of the German school system is that those who do not make the grade at school can attend the *Volkschochschule* at night and, whilst working (if they succeed in getting a job) can still continue their academic education during their apprenticeship by receiving appropriate time off. They also have the opportunity, if sufficiently motivated, to improve their qualifications through adult education, which enables students to pass a special form of *Abitur* ("Fachabitur") which entitles them to attend a polytechnic. Everything is done to encourage people to improve their education.

The 66 German universities are a mainstay of local culture, especially the old ones: Göttingen, Frankfurt, Cologne, Heidelberg and Munich. Göttingen used to be the university for the Kingdom of Hanover and housed the famous Göttingen Seven, a group of professors who in 1837 protested at the lack of freedom in the country. Munich's Ludwig-Maximilian University was first founded in Landshut when the court was there. The University of Erlangen-Nuremberg is a combination of two universities, the former originally in Bayreuth, the latter in Altdorf, where Wallenstein matriculated and was sent down for bad behaviour and Leibnitz wrote his

*Universities*

doctoral thesis. Each of the older universities has its own history and famous students.

Many new universities have sprung up to cater for the increased number of students and, in the border area in the south, prevent the population drift to the larger cities. Munich, Frankfurt and Cologne are the most popular universities and, though student numbers are falling in some faculties, others are grossly overfull. Students have to listen to lectures over loudspeakers in adjacent lecture halls. However it should be added that education is free and that university and school teachers are relatively well paid.

During the thirties academic freedom was virtually extinguished. During the sixties there were the student revolts, which led to structural changes to try and satisfy the more reasonable student demands for a say in running universities, although real power remains within the university with the professors and the administration. However, this power is itself circumscribed by that of the local Ministry of Education, itself answerable to the *Land* Parliament. In matters of policy it is the responsible official in the Ministry who decides what is to be done because he controls the money bags. Within the university itself it is the President and Registrar who decide how that money is to be spent. Accordingly universities are basically bureaucracies, and sometimes heavy-handed ones.

There are no faculty clubs or senior common rooms as in the USA and Britain respectively. There are no Junior Common Rooms or students' union buildings. There are student hostels but no American-style dorms or colleges. There is little student loyalty to the university itself, which the students regard as a career or trade school. Universities are in effect factories churning out a product, in this case job-hunters.

The catch here, however, is graduate unemployment. Many students drop out before graduating; many of these (63–68 per cent) get jobs in the belief that it is better to earn a living at a lower level than originally intended than graduate well qualified but unemployable. This is particularly so with would-be teachers. The result is to decimate some faculties and disciplines, with whole groups of students changing the course of their studies in mid-stream. This causes chaos at the universities concerned.

Accordingly there is general disillusionment with university education as an open sesame to well-salaried employment. Of course certain professions – doctors, natural scientists etc. – still take the pick of the best graduates. But a university degree no longer provides a meal ticket. Consequently unqualified job hunters coming from the less academic schools are getting squeezed out of job opportunities and are joining the unemployed at the bottom of society, with all the possibly explosive consequences involved.

German students are usually much older than their *Students* English or American counterparts when they leave university: a humanities student 26, a lawyer 27 and a medic 28-plus. This is explained by the late school-leaving age (18–19) and by the length of the study itself, which is now on average seven years! In a sense German students tend to be more mature because of their age, but on the other hand less realistic because they are privileged not to have to earn a living as they would otherwise be expected to do. 10 per cent get married at university and a significantly large percentage of couples, if they do not get married, live together. It is an adult society in an artificial environment.

The German approach to scholarship in the humani- *Scholarship* ties is more detailed, abstract and theoretical than elsewhere. German scholars are fearful of being considered simplistic. The style of language used is formal and dry. There is little, if any, humour and an abundance of footnotes. Students write seminar papers as opposed to essays. The essay as an English genre is seldom used. The humanities professors and lecturers regard themselves as, for want of a better expression, 'scientific professors', that is, scholars on a plane with their colleagues in the natural sciences. The word *Wissenschaft* (scholarship) is used in a laboratory sense. Law (*Rechtswissenschaft*), Fine Art (*Kunstwissenschaft*), History (*Geschichtswissenschaft*), even Librarianship (*Bibliothekswissenschaft*) are included.

Learning is taken desperately seriously. A professor will dissect a poem like a biologist a frog. One professor said: 'We scholars aim to understand the text better than the author.' Sometimes one has the impression that scholars go overboard, like the two professors who are supposed to have challenged one another to a duel over the verse order of the *Nibelungenlied*! Duels have long since been forbidden, but tempers do get very frayed in university seminars and the cut and thrust of academe has to be experienced to be believed. Possibly this is so the world over, though in Germany it can be pursued with an intensity which takes one's breath away. One professor advised a junior colleague, new to the professorial life, always to go around with a knife unsheathed!

*A Schein*  Certain words become key expressions in Germany: *Ausweis* (identity card) is one and *Schein* (certificate) is another. It is part of compound nouns such as *Fahrschein* (railway ticket) or *Gutschein* (credit note), but the word alone is important enough when it simply means 'a certificate' which one has earned at school or university for having passed a test or written a seminar paper. Once you have the requisite number of certificates, then you can sit for the final exam.

**The press**  The press is dominated by a few large newspaper concerns, e.g. Springer, which publishes the popular *Bild Zeitung*. There is no national quality daily paper, with the exception of the *Frankfurter Allgemeine Zeitung* published in Frankfurt. People tend to be loyal to their regional papers, like the *Süddeutsche Zeitung* in Munich, the *Stuttgarter Zeitung* in Stuttgart or the *Südwestpresse* in Ulm. The quality weekly paper *Die Zeit* is published in Hamburg by the large publishing house Gerd Bucerius, where a number of popular magazines appear. Provincial newspapers tend to be run by the larger urban dailies or by rural conglomerates producing virtually the same paper in each small town with different local news items.

In general the style of journalism is different from the English-speaking variety. The front-page foreign news is very obviously collated from the news agencies rather than from the paper's own reporters overseas. However, the inside pages do contain more interestingly written articles and reports from correspondents abroad. The arts page (*Feuilleton*) published in the weekend edition is usually excellent. There is only one Sunday newspaper (*Die Welt am Sonntag*), which is a Catholic newspaper. The Anglo-Saxon custom of reading the Sunday papers does not exist in Germany. Visitors staying in the larger cities can often obtain the London Sunday papers the same day at the main railway station. They are exceedingly expensive. The *Sunday Telegraph*, which has always been the cheapest, now costs DM 4.

The only other German-language quality newspaper is Swiss, *Die Neue Züricher Zeitung*. The style is excellent, but it is not a very exciting paper to read. German quality journalism seldom is. Newspapers inform rather than entertain. There is no humorous magazine in the same mould as *Punch*.

Satirical magazines like *Pardon* and *Titanic* certainly bite, though they are much less cruel than the British *Private Eye*. This might be connected with the fact that freedom of the press has only existed sporadically in the nineteenth and twentieth centuries. Also the law appears to afford a great deal of protection to the individual by obliging newspapers to correct factual errors by printing the dissatisfied party's version of events.

Even if one cannot read German, newspapers are useful in providing the visitor with a list of entertainment: cinema and theatre as well as exhibitions etc. Moreover, when looking for accommodation or wanting to advertise for it, buy a second-hand car or sell up old crocks before leaving the country, the local advertisements column is invaluable.

**Radio and television** Radio and television are organized regionally, with each of the *Länder* having its own broadcasting station for both. There was for some years discussion about setting up a national television station, initiated by Chancellor Konrad Adenauer. It was resisted at the time because the *Länder* feared that too much power would be assumed by the Federal Government. A compromise was reached whereby the Second German Television was founded in 1961 with it headquarters in Mainz. Its constitution, whilst seeming to ensure editorial freedom, at the same time left control with the *Länder*. The network has become the largest European television station.

Cable television has only recently been introduced and can only be viewed in some parts of the country, though more cable is being laid all the time. There was considerable opposition to the introduction of cable television for political reasons, but on the whole the idea has now been accepted.

The station RIAS Berlin is in the American sector. *Deutschlandfunk* and *Deutsche Welle* project a picture of West Germany in their programmes and provide a world service.

The individual *Länder* stations are constituted by law to preserve their freedom. Although they do maintain a high degree of editorial freedom, the choice of Director is usually influenced by the *Länder* governments.

The standard of programmes is varied. Many foreign films, especially serials, are shown, inevitably *Dallas, Falcon Crest* etc.; and latterly local productions such as the *Schwarzwaldklinik* (a hospital drama featuring a super-surgeon, Professor Brinkmann, who is a great lover too) and the *Familie Drombusch* (an everyday family). There are also the inevitable detective serials, such as *Der Kommissar* or *Der Alte*, but the standard is uneven. Pure entertainment often consists of sport coverage, the unavoidable quiz progammes and light music. Both television and radio have advertisements, which provide a source of additional revenue, most of which comes from listeners' and viewers' fees.

Undoubtedly some of the best viewing comprises

the informative programmes: news, travel and educational. Visitors can watch a 15-minute programme, *News of the Week*, in English. It is an excellent programme, produced by Bavarian Television. Radio Bavaria broadcasts the news in English and French at 9.55 a.m. every weekday. There are also schools programmes in English, broadcast in most of the *Länder*. And motorists will find the special motoring programmes useful. They are partly in English.

Just to listen to the radio or watch television offers the visitor a fairly painless way of learning about Germany. Even if one understands very little at first, one soon begins to recognize words, especially on television where the context is visually explained.

A great force in German life is the *Kleinbürger* (a member of the lower-middle or rather upper-working class, not highly educated, but articulate in making wishes and prejudices known), a force for good on the whole in helping to run a well regulated society, but possibly suspicious of too much innovation.

**The Kleinbürger**

It is people like this who run the allotment gardeners' association, the animal protection clubs, the War Veterans' and War Wounded clubs and of course the refugee organizations for those Germans who had to flee from Silesia and other parts of the former German *Reich*. They also combine together to build housing estates consisting of blocks of flats and lobby the local council for children's playgrounds, improved municipal bus services, bus shelters etc. Naturally conservative in a traditional sense, they mistrust the radical Left but also have reservations about too much power being assumed by Church and State. As a visitor to the country, one may tend not to notice the *Kleinbürger* until one sees that such people are all around. They are the real Germans, described and caricatured in Heinrich Mann's *Professor Unrat* or Heinrich Böll's *Ende einer Dienstfahrt*.

The *Kleinbürger* overlaps with, though is not always the same as, the *Beamter* (the civil servant), who has special rights and privileges. It is an offence to insult

**The Beamter**

*Beamte*; they do not have to pay contributions to their old-age pensions. They are the servants of the State, but in many respects also run it. They are the interpreters of the many regulations which seem to run every citizen's life. They have great power: they are the people who can grant or withhold certificates and permissions. The rest of the *Kleinbürger* who are not Beamte look upon them with a mixture of respect, envy and perhaps even disapproval. They think *Beamte* are accorded too much privilege and are promoted according to age rather than achievement, whilst being paid always the same even if they do as little work as possible.

Of course it is very difficult to quantify what percentage of officialdom does a decent day's work, acts responsibly towards the State and so on. But *Beamte* are confined and restricted. They earn the same salary if they work hard or not, but equally cannot sometimes earn promotion by extra effort. And they may not strike. They owe their loyalty to their master the State. There is really no true equivalent to the German *Beamter* in the English-speaking world.

*Beamte* work everywhere. They have security and ensure security for the State. They work in radio and television, that is, in jobs where not only a sense of responsibility but also creativity and vision are required. Sometimes one feels that they lack the spur of risk and lack of security which would encourage creativity and innovation.

The German *Beamter* is found in all income groups and grades and at all social levels. Hitler would never have been made Chancellor of Germany unless he had been a *Beamter* and in order to become one, he was for a time appointed to the Prussian Inland Revenue Service. One cannot just become a *Beamter*. One becomes an apprentice-*Beamter* first; then a *Beamter* on probation; and then if found worthy, and after having sworn allegiance to the Federal constitution if one is a Federal official, or to the *Land* if a regional one, one is *verbeamtet*, this is, appointed a *Beamter* for life. One could become a senior civil servant at deputy ministerial level or be a postman or engine driver.

By having *Beamter* manning the main services, the State is always assured of being able to keep the essential services running. Of course they do not always run at a profit, but they run more or less efficiently and, with the *Bundestag* (parliament) watching over them, roughly in the public interest. Indeed over 30 per cent of the members of the *Bundestag* itself are *Beamte*. Many believe that this leads to a restrictive attitude to democracy, that a *Beamter* by definition will not defend the rights of the individual against the power of the State.

This argument is also used in relation to the independence of the judiciary. Judges are all *Beamte*, chosen not from the ranks of successful experienced barristers, but selected from young law students who have just joined the legal service. Of course only those who have obtained excellent marks in their final exam are accepted for State service; none the less initially they are relatively inexperienced, both as lawyers and as people. This is obviously a very complicated question which raises fundamental issues of the quality of the judiciary, which cannot be considered adequately in a single paragraph. However, Germans are not always convinced that when it comes to having a court case against the State or one of the *Länder* the judiciary is going to go out of its way to support the rights of the individual. When judges depend for their livelihood and promotion upon the State, why should they, people ask, bite the hand that feeds them? However, it has to be said in defence of the independence of the judiciary that, particularly in the many cases brought by citizens against the Education Ministries of the *Länder*, the Ministries, i.e. the State, often lose.

# The historical legacy

A potted history of Germany would be of little use to the reader seeking to understand what he saw on visiting the country. Instead we will concentrate on certain fundamental points of Germany's evolution to commercial leadership of the Common Market.

The history of Germany is the struggle for unity within a conglomerate of disparate groups. In England hundreds of years ago there were the different kingdoms of Mercia, Northumbria, etc.; in Germany these kingdoms, principalities, duchies and city states existed well into the nineteenth century. Napoleon radically reduced the number in 1804, and Bismarck created the German Empire in 1871, but it still contained a surprising number of constituent states until 1918.

**Religion** Since the Reformation, religion has created a geographical and psychological division between the Protestant north of Germany and the Roman Catholic south. This division was intensified in the seventeenth century by the Thirty Years' War, which brought pillage, massacre and rape to the whole of central Europe, and greatly affected Germany's social and economic development.

Secularization, that is, the expropriation of (Catholic) Church lands and property by the State, occurred very late in Germany, in 1804. Consequently the Church, that is the Pope, often had considerable influence in the south, and could not be ignored in the north either, as Bismarck's differences with Rome show. The compromise which was ultimately reached between Bismarck and the Pope, and which is still observed today, left temporal power with the State (formerly individual states), in return for the Church, both Catholic and Protestant, retaining certain privileges, in particular the payment of *Kirchensteuer* (8–9 per cent tax on every working citizen's earnings, depending upon which of the *Länder* he lives in).

Today in the north the Church does not appear to have as much influence as in the south (particularly in Bavaria), where the Roman Catholic Church is very influential in education. However, sometimes this degree of influence is disruptive because of the resentment it causes among those who seek to secularize education still further – that is, to exclude religious instruction from the classroom.

Thus the Church still makes its voice heard even though fewer people now go to church. There is a Catholic univeristy (Eichstätt) in Bavaria, but the Bavarian Government is very careful to maintain a balance in State patronage by also supporting universities in Protestant areas.

## Struggle for freedom and democracy

It is reckoned that there are some 2000 political prisoners in East German prisons. It would be extraordinary if the average West German's political awareness were not influenced by this stark reality.

The struggle for freedom and democracy is a very chequered one because it became entangled, indeed strangled, by Bismarck's struggle for German supremacy. The revolution of 1848 produced the Frankfurt Parliament, but this floundered because it lacked military teeth and a sense of unity. Ultimately Bismarck's victory over Austria, Hanover and Bavaria in 1866 assured Prussian dominance within Germany, and in 1871 King William of Prussia became Emperor of the new German Empire. Prussian society was based on a caste system which projected a rigid, hierarchical way of thinking.

Although Bismarck was a bitter opponent of Socialism and tried unsuccessfully to ban the party with an anti-socialist law which the *Reichstag* (Parliament) refused to pass, he introduced workers' health and insurance schemes which were milestones in social welfare and can be said to have inaugurated the welfare state. But welfare was not to be equated with freedom. Germany only obtained universal suffrage after the First World War during the short-lived

Weimar Republic, which itself yielded to Hitler. Only after the war did Germany take the first steps in walking along the road to freedom; and, without being patronizing, she has made truly remarkable progress since then.

If German history tells us anything, it is surely that the whole context of religious strife and struggle for national unity which fettered personal freedom never gave democracy a chance. The fact that while West Germany has thrown off her chains the East should be more securely shackled than ever, is the tragic but one hopes not the final irony of German history.

**Civil courage and resistance to Hitler** Civil courage has not always been a German virtue. Traditionally it was virtuous to obey, and preserve the status quo. Loyalty to the King, the Emperor, the State and hence to the *Führer* was the eleventh commandment.

Nevertheless, there *were* individual Germans who resisted Hitler – perhaps not very many, but precisely because there were so few, they were all the more remarkable: the student brother-and-sister pair, Hans and Inge Scholl (called the White Rose Movement), Count von Stauffenberg, who unsuccessfully tried to dispose of Hitler in July 1944, the Jewish nun Edith Stein and Pastor Martin Niemöller.

**Post-war Germany** The great problem in the post-war period was to put Germany on her feet again without endangering the hard-won peace of Europe: to allow them to rise again but peacefully, to reform without exciting resentment (no second Versailles!) and – as time went on – to use her as a buffer against possible Soviet expansionism. Whether all the managers of German resurrection and reconstruction realized this is another question. Circumstances determined the general direction: the twin desires to reform and reconstruct were sometimes at variance with one another. Shipping off whole factories to Britain seemed vengeful, although this encouraged local investment in new machinery. What the West saw as the Russian threat concentrated everybody's minds: the Americans helped with the Marshall Plan, the

British and French supported General Lucius Clay's refusal to budge on Berlin.

The American influence in Germany is visible in dress and on television, audible on the radio and in record shops and apparent in industry and commerce. Apart from the fact that every fourth American is of German immigrant descent, there are undeniably basic American-German affinities. Both are now unconstrained by social tradition. Both have the same go-getting, thrusting approach to business.

**The American influence**

Most Germans will admit that the Allied presence in the post-war period was beneficial, indeed crucial, to the birth and existence as well as to the prosperity of the country. Many feel that the American presence has now become an embarrassment, particularly the war-heads on German soil. Whereas some politicians see American armaments as guaranteeing continued peace, others regard their being kept on German soil as a provocation to the Soviet Union.

The past has been neither forgotten nor forgiven by some Jews, but somehow philosophically mastered by others. The explosion of anti-semitism during Hitler's Reich remains inexplicable in its expression, so utterly contrary to the German character as regards order, rectitude and (one has to add) cleanliness – the concentration camps were filthy. The treatment of the Jews represented a mental aberration.

**Germany and the Jews**

The problem exercises many people's minds, particularly when anniversaries occur of this or that outrage, or when Israeli leaders visit the Federal Republic. There are arguments as to whether or not one can talk of national or merely generation guilt; debates over the extent to which the sins of individuals can stain a whole nation after decades.

The suicide of Rudolf Hess, Hitler's deputy, raised such questions yet again, and the scenes in Wunsiedel where neo-Nazis protested about not being allowed to pay their respect disturbed and revolted many people. One German paper refused to report any-

thing more about Hess than that he had died. It
refused to concern itself with such a person any more.

German Jewry lives on. Around 27,000 Jews are
now living in the Federal Republic, and around 600 in
the German Democratic Republic. Documentary
films on television show interviews with American
Jews, some of whom utterly condemn, others refuse
to condemn, all Germans for the horrors of the past.

**The status of
Berlin**

Although Bonn is the Federal capital, West German
politicians have a special loyalty to Berlin and always
try and incorporate it into national events, much to
the annoyance of the German Democratic Republic,
which proclaims East Berlin as its own capital city.

Bonn used to be referred to as the *Regierungsdorf*
(government village), but now the building of an
airport, new offices for the Federal Chancellor and
other government offices and the cosmopolitan
atmosphere generated by the diplomatic corps have
all created the atmosphere of a capital city. It is any
case near Cologne, a major cultural and industrial
centre.

Berlin is in many respects a ghost capital, isolated
by surrounding East German territory and only
joined to the rest of the Federal Republic by an air
corridor and the right of access along the motorways.
Officially the four Allied Powers are responsible for
the city. In fact the Russians leave running East Berlin
to the East German Government and the Western
Allies the administration of West Berlin to the West
Germans.

The Federal President has a villa in the city, and the
State insurance scheme for employees as well as a
number of other federal agencies have their headquarters there. Firms basing themselves there enjoy special
privileges and reductions. There are even tax deduc-
tions for certain forms of investment in Berlin. Berlin
children are offered holidays in the rest of the Federal
Republic. West German and foreign visitors and
students are able to enjoy subsidized visits to the city.

It is a divided city with two sovereign flags waving
in it. Whilst the East German Berliners can move
about within their own country, West Berliners need

visas to leave the city. Apart from the real locals who do not feel the need to see other parts of the country, most people are forever catching planes or on the move to get out of the city, otherwise life becomes too claustrophobic.

The 750th anniversary highlighted the discordances between East and West whilst drawing attention to Germany's national heritage.

Whilst in their heart of hearts many West Germans undoubtedly feel a sincere loyalty towards West Berlin, some of them find the whole precarious status and existence of the city dangerously embarrassing. One should remember that although Berlin was the German capital, it was so for only 74 years; and in any case regionalism prevented it having the significance for Germans that capital cities often have elsewhere.

One associates with Germans for historical reasons an inability to compromise. Nothing could be further from the truth today. The essence of the German spirit of negotiation is to find a modus vivendi. This can be observed in Germany's foreign policy, which basically is one of supporting the USA without antagonizing the Soviet Union, placating Israel without annoying the Arab states, carrying on trade with South Africa whilst giving considerable help to the Third World, essentially leading Europe without trying to dominate it. The most difficult part of all constitutes relations with the German Democratic Republic: trying to obtain some measure of reform without appearing to interfere, and virtually buying improved treatment of East Germans and West German visitors to the GDR with extended credits and other commercial inducements. The Federal Government's foreign policy under Hans-Dietrich Genscher is carried out with consummate skill. It would be disastrous for West Germany to act differently, because her room for manoeuvre is so narrow. What extends it is her increasing wealth.

Germans generally in business and in official dealings prefer compromise because it is the best way, be it in resolving the numerous post-war scandals of

**The will to compromise**

banks collapsing or of politicians being accused of misuse of their official power. In a case like the AEG (Allgemeine Elektrizitäts-Gesellschaft) bankruptcy, which can pose a considerable financial threat to the community, the State steps in, an expensive rescue operation is mounted and the general public does not suffer widespread unemployment or ruin. What really decides things is not what happens officially in public, but behind the scenes in private, where the dealing goes on. Similarly within a German organization: if you want something, you go to the official or manager concerned and work it out with him. The written word is purely confirmatory.

# Festivals and customs

Festivals are traditionally connected with particular times of year and particular crafts. Whilst today many people regard them as holidays from work and an excuse to eat sausage and drink beer, historically they had a deeper significance – although by all accounts vast quantities of sausage and beer were also consumed on such occasions in the past.

Many festivals are of religious origin. As Germany is roughly divided between the Protestant north and the Catholic south, even the religiously based festivals and customs differ, quite apart from the local ones. It is therefore difficult to talk of national folklore because it is essentially regional, though of course the Oberammergau Passion Play, for example, is of international renown. However, it is unlikely that north Germans would have heard of the *Fürstenhochzeit* in Landshut (an annual festival celebrating the marriage between the Polish king's daughter Hedwig and the Bavarian duke's son George). A few years ago all the historic costumes were burnt, which was a Bavarian tragedy.

Germany has a particularly strong tradition of rural culture, in regional folklore, customs, music and art. Well into the nineteenth and the beginning of the twentieth century Germany had an essentially agricultural economy. Over 50 per cent of the country is still arable, although most of the population now lives in urban areas. The move from the land continues to this day.

German life is rich in customs. They are part of everyday life. For example, one could be walking along the street and see a group of building workers in their Sunday best being played to by a band on top of an uncompleted building. The roof is on but not covered with slates and tiles. Right on top you see what looks like a small Christmas tree with white or coloured streamers attached to it floating in the breeze. Speeches are being made and every now and again you can hear cheers wafted down from a great height. The builders are of course celebrating the roof going up which, after all, is what is considered to be the decisive moment in building a house.

**Christmas**    It is not the custom to send Christmas cards to all one's acquaintances. One usually only sends them to the nearest and dearest, although some firms send them pro forma to customers. When in doubt, don't. You will save yourself considerable trouble and not force the recipient to feel obliged to return the compliment. The same goes for Easter. Writing is usually kept either for business or for very close friends or relations. The telephone has swept all before it, particularly after the introduction of cheap night and weekend rates. You often hear people say: 'I don't have any time to write.'

The main feast day is not Christmas day itself, but Christmas Eve (*Heilige Abend*). Shops shut at 12 noon and then everybody rushes home to celebrate an essentially family affair. Most young people visit their parents on this day and many then go skiing on Christmas Day. The day following Christmas Day is just referred to as the second Christmas holiday, and has no special name.

Christmas is also a time when older people think of their parents who have left for a better world. One sees the graveyards full of people paying their respects to the departed. A married couple will visit the graves of both sets of parents. German Catholics also visit family graves on All Saints' Day, and they are punctilious in the way they tend the graves.

Nothing is taken lightly in Germany, and the joy of Christmas is muted by reflection. One listens to a Christmas poem on the radio in between Advent songs and carols. The poem might, for instance, tell the story of a devout and conscientious village crib maker who enjoins his sons, when he is gone, to continue the good work he has done. He goes to the church to repair some of the figures and fails to return. On opening the church the next morning, his sons find the old man seemingly asleep after devoutly watching the crib. Of course he is dead.

In most German towns there is a *Christkindelsmarkt* (Christ-Child Market) from the end of November every day up to Christmas Eve. The most famous one is in Nuremberg, where in the central market place there is a crib and a choir with musicians. Carols are sung to the crowds which throng the market buying a profusion of sweets, special Christmas biscuits, hot sizzling sausages and other warm meats from the market stalls. In Nuremberg one can see everything without being crushed in the crowds by walking along the terrace which runs along one side of the street. On the other side of the market place there is the fountain with a 'magic' ring, which those with a secret wish may touch and be appropriately rewarded.

*Christkin-delsmarkt*

Incidentally, Nuremberg, the historic centre of which was bombed in the war, has been beautifully restored, so that a walk through the old cobbled streets and across the river is an experience on its own.

Christmas is glorious and for an English observer complicated. Father Christmas is the *Weihnachts-mann* who fixes children up with toys at Christmas. However, in the south it is the Christ Child who brings presents. Presents are piled round the Christmas tree and opened on Christmas Eve.

*Father Christmas and Co.*

On 6 December a different character, Nikolaus, dressed in Father Christmas-like clothes, appears with a servant called Rupprecht, who is usually dark-complexioned and spanks naughty children with an old broom. Afterwards Nikolaus distributes presents to the children, including the reprobates. Nikolaus and Rupprecht are not meant to frighten children, but to be a friendly yet firm reminder to both children and grown-ups.

As if this were not enough, there are the Three Kings, usually represented by children dressed in white with moustaches stuck on their upper lips and faces smeared in grease paint or charcoal. They appear at one's front door around 6 January carrying a cross and sing a carol (often fairly indifferently). Their aim is not simply religious (if at all), but mercenary. They want money to buy sweets or some other minor luxuries. They are really in the same category as the 'trick-or-treat' kids and can be avoided by simply not opening the door.

**Fasching**   *Fasching* (carnival) is celebrated with great gusto in the south, especially in Bavaria. Each city, town and village has its own prince and princes and, where it can be afforded, a guard of pretty girls. There are processions to open the carnival and in the larger cities and towns different professions, crafts and guilds hold their own balls and parties. Celebrations last from 7 January to Shrove Tuesday.

People dress up in carnival costume. It is as the Germans say, 'die Narrenzeit' (the time for fools). The general purpose is to be merry and assume another role; some parties are riotous. Do join in, if you are invited; or risk going to the public balls, for which entrance is charged. Even if it is not quite your scene, it is very interesting to see German *Sie's* becoming *Du's* and behaving with suitable abandon. Mates are lost and new ones found, or people just have an excuse to get sozzled. It is fun on Shrove Tuesday to go into government offices, even post offices, and see everyone in carnival costume. If you are in Munich, you can join the market women dancing in the streets. It gives one a new insight into the German way of life (or forgetting and enjoying it) and suggests that perhaps the Germans do not take life so seriously after all.

**Other festivals**   There are more specialized festivals, like the five-day annual Cologne Carnival with the spectacular Rose Monday Parade; the Mainz *Fastnacht*, which originally parodied the old monarchy and is held from 7 January till Shrove Tuesday; and the Oberammergau Passion Play held every seven years (next one in 1991). There is a whole provincial tradition of passion of which Oberammergau is the most famous. German literature, like English, is also rich in Easter drama. The story of the Pied Piper is re-enacted in Hamelin every Sunday at noon from the middle of May to mid-September. And of course one should not forget the Munich October Beer Festival (*Oktoberfest*).

Some Germans wear national dress not only on Sundays and for tourist cameras, but as part of their folklore and to work on the land, even to work in the city. Bavarian women wear Dirndl dresses, the men *Janker* (jackets), *Lodenmantel* (overcoats) and even *Lederhosen* (short leather trousers) as normal every-day wear, like a Scot wearing his kilt in Scotland. **National dress**

# Health and sport

Health and sport go together in Germany. People suffered great deprivation during and immediately after the last war. Many overcompensated afterwards and became overweight; and now have become health-conscious because of the new awareness of heart trouble. Jogging is not as popular as in the United States, but people of all age groups do it. The Germans have a tradition of being health enthusiasts, one could say cranks; one thinks of Gaylord Hauser, the vegetarian, and Father Kneipp, famous for his water cure.

**Taking the Kur**

It is a longstanding German institution for all classes to go on a *Kur*, that is, spending six weeks or more having treatment at a health resort or spa for a particular illness, disability or condition. There is a whole *Kur*-tradition in Germany described by celebrated novelists; an example is Thomas Mann's *Der Zauberberg*.

Opinions differ as to the efficacy of taking the *Kur*. Certainly in the nineteenth century, taking the *Kur* was basically a social event. Bismarck was at Bad Ems when he sent the famous despatch which provoked the Franco-Prussian War, and Edward VII went to rest his overindulged body at Bad Homburg.

Today the social part still continues, but unofficially, and very much down the social ladder. The *Kur* is certainly not a holiday for the participants – in some cases extremely energetic and demanding treatment is offered. This can include early-morning *Fango* treatment (being covered in warm peat or mud, then finally washed clean and rested) before submitting to the ordeal of drinking the local spa water, the mineral content of which is supposed to contain many health-giving properties but usually excludes any suggestion of a pleasant taste. Massages, exercises, walks and rest follow, interspersed with diet-controlled meals.

It is perhaps the diet which is most helpful, as well as the opportunity to go for walks in the usually pleasantly wooded and rural surroundings. Of course many *Kur* patients lack self-discipline and are too hedonistic to submit to an all-too monastic existence. They lead a vigorous social life and patronize local cafés, restaurants and dance halls. They also drive their own cars, which is specifically forbidden.

*Kuren* are big business for spas and cost the health insurance schemes considerable sums of money. Whether the whole exercise is worth it, from, the health point of view, is debatable. What is certain is that people get away from work for six weeks and then return home to enjoy the *Nach-Kur* (post-cure), which is intended to enable the patient to readjust to daily life.

## Smoking

With thousands dying every year from lung cancer in the Federal Republic, people have become more aware of the dangers of smoking. Non-smoking areas or tables now exist in some restaurants and canteens. Smoking is forbidden in cinemas, in the underground and is discouraged on buses and trams. Smoking still remains a problem for a non-smoker in pubs, where the 'air' is thick with smoke, and one returns home with one's clothes still reeking of the fug. All one can say is that the Federal Ministry of Health is adopting measures to protect the non-smoker and smoking is being forbidden in government offices. However – and this may seem absurd, even morally reprehensible – hospitals still allow smoking. This is a very difficult problem to resolve to everybody's satisfaction, because Germans for historical reasons are very fussy about preserving personal freedom. Smokers feel that they have a right to smoke, regardless of the health hazards involved for themselves or others.

## Absence of prudery

On the whole one can say that Germans have an uncomplicated and natural attitude to sex. Pornographic literature is allowed and sold openly, sex shops ply their wares prominently at international airports and less so in small cities. In general everybody just gets on with it because, within the very flexible limits of respectability, it is regarded as a perfectly natural form of human activity.

Where, however, passions have been aroused is in the debate over amending paragraph 218 of the Criminal Code concerning abortion, which is now legalized within the first twelve weeks where rape or the like has occurred or later on where the life of the mother is endangered. This has caused considerable conscience-searching among prelates and politicians and has accordingly widened for a time the differences between Protestants and Catholics. The latter remain adamant against abortion, even where the life of the mother is endangered.

Homosexuality between consenting adults is legalized according to paragraph 175 of the Criminal Code. The age of consent is 18. Homosexual relations between adults and children are forbidden.

Another source of controversy is the problem of whether or not to include sex as a subject in schools. Many parents resent the State assuming the right to explain something so intimate as sex in school. They regard this as an invasion of parental authority.

*AIDS*   It was reckoned that in 1987 some 800 people of the Federal Republic had contracted AIDS, and half of them were already dead. Nobody knows how many carriers there are. After a nationwide debate it was recently decided by the Federal Minister of Health not to have compulsory registration of AIDS sufferers. This may change. Prostitutes report a falling-off of business, at the same time however a stubborn refusal by clients to use condoms. Business prospects are bleak for the oldest profession in the world, which in Germany, where everything is officially registered and put down in black and white, means a dwindling of tax revenue. Prostitutes have to be officially registered, must report to local Medical Officers of Health for checkups and must pay taxes. Bureaucracy is involved here, it would appear, for everybody's benefit.

Homosexual prostitutes report a falling-off of business too. Their red-light districts in the larger cities are well-known to the initiated. Homosexual magazines like *DU* and *DON* give the requisite information in their advertisement columns.

**Sport**

Sport in Germany is a substitute for patriotism, which has otherwise disappeared. It has a mystic quality about it. The most unathletic, non-sporty looking people cheer on tennis stars. Germany is seasonally sports mad. Walk the streets during the equivalent of a soccer cup final and you will be alone, every now and again hearing cheers or groans from excited viewers huddled in front of their television screens.

Sport often brings out the best in Germans. They commit fewer fouls on the football field than British players and their youth goes less often on the rampage than in the United Kingdom. Seldom, if ever, have German supporters abroad ever made a nuisance of themselves. Germans are basically very well behaved. When Germany wins an international

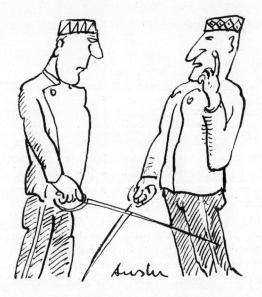

*'I'd like it about here, please.'*

cup there is national rejoicing. Germans are noble in defeat and generous in victory.

Sport is a harmless national mania of which there are many forms and varieties, some of them regionalized like Bavarian *Fingerhakeln* (finger tug) or, if you can call this sport, seeing who can take the most snuff! Hunting on horseback is forbidden. There is no fox-hunting, except mock hunts where horse and hounds follow a rider trailing a dead fox or the tail of one on his arm. Wild boar hunting with guns is popular in the country and it is done on foot. German horsemanship is of the highest standard as is shown at national equestrian events.

**Skiing** The enthusiasm for sport is infectious and widespread. Skiing and ice hockey make sport an all-the-year-round occupation. High in the Swiss Alps, as opposed to the German or Austrian Alps, one can ski in the spring (sometimes even in the summer). Skiing is not exclusively a sport for southerners. North Germans ski too, as the number of cars travelling south on the motorway with skis aboard shows. Early on a winter Sunday morning you see skiers off for a day in the mountains. These tough young, middle-aged and even senior-looking people are quite undeterred by the cold or the long wait for a ski lift. The whole gives the impression of a non-stop circus, with hordes of people in multi-coloured attire cascading down the freezing slopes. When the sun finally comes out and some warmth is generated the grim cold yields to a truly festive atmosphere. People relax, icy faces turn to warm smiles, and as the church bells ring for midday, some people go off for lunch in the various restaurants down below or in the *Almhütte* on top of the mountain. One cannot deny how picturesque some ski resorts are and how seductively soothing the *Glühwein* (hot spiced wine) tastes. People remove their anoraks and the odd sweater, loosen their ski boots and relax. The noise can be deafening, the fug impenetrable but everybody is enjoying themselves before the somewhat more relaxed afternoon skiing to come. When the sun sinks on the horizon people have already left the slopes, fixed skis onto their luggage racks and, after scraping the frost off their window screens, started on the bumper-to-bumper trek home.

The larger sports shops, like Sport-Scheck and Münzinger in Munich, run weekend ski courses, and parents find this a good way of getting rid of their high-spirited children while they either stay at home or ski at a more leisurely pace.

The sport becomes a way of life for the whole family. It keeps them fit, apart from the odd broken leg, which is a sign of sportsmanship (the broken ski is kept as a souvenir, the leg carefully reset and the resultant hobbling and inconvenience cheerfully born).

Cross-country skiing is also very popular and the routes are well selected and marked out to enable the skier to enjoy the snow-clad fields and forests. The skis used for cross-country skiing are shorter than those used for skiing downhill. Equipment (skis, ski sticks and boots) can usually be hired at resorts, but if you intend to ski a lot it is obviously better to invest in at least your own ski boots.

If you are taking a skiing holiday, go easy on the skiing for the first day or two after arrival. The temptation is to do too much in the first joy and excitement. Easy does it, and never get foolhardy. It is worth learning the mountain code.

It is advisable to join a ski class. Some teachers are better than others, so see which one fits your personality best. It is not always the younger, more dashing teacher who makes the best or most patient instructor.

The main problem with skiing is keeping warm. The temperature on the mountain slopes is often glacial, certainly freezing and it can be very cold going up the mountain slope on an open chair lift. If one is frozen on reaching the top and then begins to ski down the slope without one's body being properly warm, relaxed and supple, this is when accidents can occur. It is absolutely essential to wrap up well.

Before setting out on a skiing expedition, it is

always as well to listen to weather reports on the radio, which may include special advice for skiers.

*Avalanches*   When skiing it really is advisable to observe to the letter any instructions given regarding avoiding probable or existing avalanches. It is a very unpleasant death to be suffocated in an avalanche. There are always people who disregard warnings. If you are going on a long ski tour, always ask first about possible avalanches.

It may be that whilst driving in the mountains, the road may suddenly become blocked by an avalanche ahead. Turn back if you can. Temperatures drop rapidly at night, and it is easily possible to freeze to death.

**Sunday afternoons – walking**   Germans love their cars, but they are equally keen on walking, and there is a ritual about the Sunday-after-lunch walk. The whole family sets out, often in their Sunday best, in the direction of a café where, after healthy exercise, coffee and cakes (the latter with whipped cream) can be eaten with a fairly clear conscience.

Walking or rather rambling is a way of life for many people, especially in the mountains. It awakens inherent feelings of getting back to nature, which so often have to be sacrificed in this automobile and generally polluted age. Some Germans are great climbers and mountaineers. Whilst you will not be expected to climb the Alps, you may well be invited to accompany everybody on a country walk. Take sensible clothes and be prepared. You may well be in for a fairly strenuous time.

# Agriculture and industry

West Germany is now the largest exporter in the world (overtaking the USA in 1987). However, whilst the popular mountain summer-holiday and winter-sports resorts attract more visitors every year, the number of those who derive their living from the land itself is falling.

When visiting some parts of Germany you might be taken with the old-fashioned and romantic-looking peasants tilling the fields, the men weather-beaten and purposefully clad, the women often in old-fashioned garb. Isn't it wonderful to see that sort of thing in the twentieth century, you might think to yourself as you settle back in the comfortable *TEE-Zug* purring along the railway tracks. The sun is shining, the train attendant brings you an expensive plastic mug of coffee and you have a perfect combination of the old and new, history (or relics thereof) and progress.

**Problems of agriculture**

Leave the train and talk to the peasant farmers and you will get a shock. They are not the jolly peasants you might imagine but a hard-working family scratching a living from a smallholding, with the husband probably just spending a few hours of his free time (he has a job in the local town) to help his wife and mother work the land. The problem is first that he, Herr Schulz the small farmer, does not get enough for his produce; second that his smallholding, like many others, is too small – on an average 12 to 15 hectares (30–37 acres) – to make it economic under present conditions; third that German agriculture as a whole is producing too much to sell; and finally that within the Common Market, German agricultural products are too expensive to compete.

Economically speaking, the solution would be to

pension Herr Schulz off and combine his and his friends' smallholdings into one anonymous large holding, employing a faceless manager and expensive machinery. If you did that of course Herr Schulz and those like him would lose whichever government introduced such measures the next election. So things things remain much as they are, with constant bickering interspersed with government speakers saying how much they treasure the farmers but regret how expensive their products are and how difficult it is to sell them.

Nevertheless, things are changing gradually. In the Federal Republic the number of farms has declined by 41 per cent since 1965 and in Bavaria by 31 per cent, where 96 per cent of the land is devoted to farm land and market gardens. Whilst at the turn of the century one farmer fed four people, he now feeds 50.

There are different structures of farming in the south and the north. Whereas in the north the farm traditionally passes to the oldest son on the death of the owner, in the south it is divided up amongst the children. Interestingly enough, in Rhineland-Westphalia the farm is taken over by the youngest son of the family, whilst the oldest son is assured of the best education that the family can afford.

The system in the south has resulted in a profusion of uneconomic smallholdings. These are now being reorganized and reduced in number in accordance with, for example, the Bavarian Ministry of Agriculture's *Flurreinigung* programme. Scattered smallholdings belonging to the same family are, with the owner's consent, being grouped together (i.e. some of the holdings are exchanged with other families' equally uneconomically scattered holdings). The consolidation of their farms makes it possible for farmers to use large agricultural machinery such as combine harvesters, and farmers are also being urged to share expensive machinery.

Rationalization has brought its own problems. Clearing away the hedgerows to allow the use of large machinery has destroyed wildlife habitats and disturbed the ecology. It has also made the countryside less attractive to visitors, who are now faced with vast

areas of monotonous single-crop farming, making
farms look like factories.

Everybody knows that West Germany is one of the **Problems of**
most prosperous countries in the world, has the **industry**
lowest rate of inflation, enjoys industrial peace and is
the world's largest exporter of manufactured goods.
Go for a walk in any German village or small town
and you will see new houses or freshly painted old
ones, new cars in the garages and every sign of
prosperity. Nobody seems to be starving. Indeed
many people are too over-weight. The economic
miracle is still in full swing.

However, appearances are not everything. The
unemployment rate is high. Traditional industries
(ship building, coal and steel) in the north are in dire
trouble, if not dying on their feet. The present lies
with automobile manufacturers and the future with
the high-tech industries, together with the aircraft
and aerospace industries, all situated in the south. It is

*'You can't beat idling about in a place where everyone works hard.'*

significant that Franz Josef Strauß, Bavaria's Minister President, pilots his own plane. Moreover, the European Patent Office is in Munich, the capital of Bavaria.

However serious its own internal readjustment problems are, West Germany remains the richest and most prosperous member of the European Common Market, of which it has assumed economic leadership. Industrial peace is partially assured by the small number of unions in existence. The largest, with some 8 million, is the Deutsche Gewerkschaftsbund (DGB), which is a conglomeration of 17 single unions representing different industrial groups independent of the type of work done. Thus unions include both white-collar executives and blue-collar workers in their membership. The advantage of this is that when it comes to wage bargaining between employers and employees, only one union is involved. Wages and salaries are then negotiated at Federal level. A Federal tariff is then agreed to, which lays down a Federal salary and wage level so that an executive worker in Hamburg is paid the same basic salary as in Munich. Even if a category of employee is not covered by the union which has negotiated the wage tariff, an employer of workers in that category may none the less pay them according to the Federal tariff.

Although on the whole the German economy is blest with amenable trade unions, the SPD (Social Democratic Party) opposition argues that economic prosperity for the few is achieved at the expense of an increasingly high proportion of the population which is sinking into relative poverty. The level of recent bankruptcies (and consequent family tragedies) is high.

The basic problem is that although productivity is increasing, it does not keep pace with increasing labour costs. Where it does, this is at the expense of increased unemployment. Automation saves industries and puts people out of work.

Moreover, costs are far lower in Japan and South Korea and the quality of those countries' products for German producers embarrassingly and for German consumers attractively high. Imports of Japanese cars and South Korean software are rising. The great question is, can West Germany meet the challenge through superior quality and new technology? At present no one can tell.

Furthermore there are two troublesome legacies of Germany's rapidly obtained prosperity.

At the height of the influx of immigrant workers from Italy, Turkey and Greece in 1979 every thirteenth person living in the Federal Republic was a foreigner. Germany, with its high wages and well developed welfare state facilities, was the promised land. At first the immigrants (euphemistically called *Gastarbeiter* – guest workers) were welcome, although often treated as second-class citizens. During the boom period they provided a workforce for the less attractive jobs. As the boom turned into a slump, provoked by the fuel crisis, and unemployment rates rose, the *Gastarbeiter* constituted a social problem. *Gastarbeiter*

There had always been a degree of prejudice against *Gastarbeiter* and there had already been integration problems – mainly cultural: language difficulties at school and jealousy amongst teenagers. Moreover, immigrants usually live in the poorer districts, where they tend to form close-knit communities. Some ugly scenes have occurred, but mercifully there have been no actual riots. Whilst there is no race discrimination act (everybody's rights are guaranteed by the Bill of Rights, i.e. *Grundgesetz*), civil good sense and restraint have paid off. And the paying-off has been in kind, with the acceptance of a government repatriation scheme to encourage guest workers to return home.

Anxiety about the environment led to the creation of a new party: the Greens. The environment has become a politically explosive issue, with activists trying to prevent extensions to Frankfurt Airport in 1979 and latterly protesting against nuclear power stations, especially Brockdorf and Wackersdorf. Indeed since Chernobyl environmental concern has come to dominate political discussion because of the immediate effect of such disasters; the temporary *The environment* pollution of the Rhine by a Swiss factory brought home to Germans the immediate effect of pollution. People find it dangerous to use tap water, the trees wither because of acid rain and even the air itself becomes so polluted that children are sent home from school.

Smog is a problem in some industrial cities and country towns on the border with the GDR and Czechoslovakia, where brown coal factories are not fitted with filters. However, international agreements have now been made with these countries to limit toxic emissions.

The visitor will not usually be affected by environmental problems, but it is worth being aware of their existence. There is a price to pay for everything. West Germany's economic miracle is no exception.

# Useful addresses

*West
Germany*

In London

German National Tourist Board/Office
61 Conduit Street
London W1R OEN
Phone: (01) 734 2600

German Tourist Facilities Ltd
184/186 Kensington Church Street
London W8 4DP
Phone: (01) 229 2474
Telex: 263696

(Cruising holidays)
Longship Holidays DFDS Travel Centre
199 Regent Street
London W1R 7WA
Phone: (01) 434 1523
Telex: 8955544

In the USA

German National Tourist Office
747 Third Avenue, 33rd floor
New York, NY 10017
Phone: (212) 308–3300

German National Tourist Office
444 South Flower Street, Suite 2230
Los Angeles CA 90071
Phone: (213) 688–7332

In Tokyo   Deutsches Kultur-Zentrum (OAG-Haus)
           7–5–56, Akasáka, Kinato-ku
           Tokyo 107
           Phone: (03) 586–0380


In Germany   German Hotel Reservation Service
             Beethovenstraße 69
             D-600 Frankfurt/Main
             Phone: (069) 740767
             Telex: 4–16 666
                 Do not dial the first 0 when phoning from outside
                 the Federal Republic of Germany.

             Mitfahrzentrale
             Hamburg:              Phone: 040 331914
             Frankfurt:            Phone: 069 230291
             Munich:               Phone: 089 280124
             Berlin:               Phone: 030 6936095


*East
Germany*

In London   Berolina Travel Limited
            Tourist Office of the GDR
            22 Conduit Street
            London W1R 9TD
            Phone: (01) 629 1664
            Telex: 263944


In Berlin   (Tourist office)
            Reisebüro der DDR
            Charlottenstraße 45
            GDR–108 Berlin

            (hotel reservations)
            International Sales
            Friedrichstraße 150153
            DDR–1080 Berlin
            Phone: 2204207 & 2204327
            Telex: 114143

British Overseas Trade Board                    **Exports to**
1–19 Victoria Street                            **Germany**
London SW1H OET
Phone: (01) 215 7877

US Department of Commerce
International Trade Administration
Washington, DC 20230


*Lufthansa*                                     **Airlines**
28 Piccadilly
London W1
Phone: (01) 408 0322

*British Airways*
75 Regent Street
London W1
Phone (reservations): (01) 370 5411

# Index

Note: References are to West Germany, except where otherwise specified.

newspapers, 37, 112–13
    advertisements in, 97, 98
    avoid taking to East Germany, 103
    delivery of, 55
    Hess not mentioned in, 121–2
    letters not sent to, 64
Niemöller, Pastor Martin, 120
night school, 109
Nikolaus, 127
noise, 42–4
non-payers of tickets, 24
'Nordsee' restaurant, 32
North-Rhine-Westphalia, 5
nuclear power stations, 141–2
Nuremberg
    Christkindelsmarkt in, 127
    toys from, 50
    Transport Museum, 9
    visiting Berlin from, 105
Nymphenburger porcelain, 49

obergärig beer, 35
Obstkuchen (fruit tart), 37
Ochsenschwanzsuppe (soup), 30
offene Wein (wine), 33
office hours, 68
Oktoberfest (beer festival), 129
Oktoberfestsbiere (beer), 35
orderliness see cleanliness and
    neatness
Ordnungsamt, 67
Osterfestsbiere (beer), 35
overcoat ritual, 76–7

parcels, charges for delivery of, 52,
    65–6
Pardon (magazine), 113
Parkhäuser (parking garages), 23
parking, 11, 23
parties see meals, invitations and
    parties
passport needed to prove identity,
    13, 25, 66, 105
patriotism, sport as substitute for, 92,
    133
Pauschalzahlung (monthly payment),
    40

payment see costs/charges
pedestrians, 18
Pensionen, booking accommodation
    at, 9
pensioners, concessionary fares for, 9
Pergamon Museum, 101
permission, 63
petrol, 104
Pflaumenkuchen (plum flan), 38
photography, 103
Pilgerfahrten (pilgrimages), 25
Pilsner/Pils (beer), 35
pizzerias, 32
platters, wooden, 50
playgrounds, 45
pleasure and work, separation of,
    86–7
plumbing, 41, 43–6
    noise of, 43–4
Poland, 94
police
    fines, 22, 23, 104
    relationship of people with, 64
political prisoners in East Germany,
    119
politics, discussing, 100–1
pollution, 142
porcelain, 49, 50, 102
pornography, 131
Portugieser Weissherbst (wine), 34
Post Office, 59–60, 65–6
    in East Germany, 99–100
Potsdam, 99, 101
Prädikat, 34
Praktischer Arzt (general
    practitioner), 61
Pralinen (chocolates), 73
preparation for travel, 12; see also
    travel
prices see costs/charges
privacy, 84
professionalism and education, 82–3
Promille (millilitres of alcohol in
    blood), 22
propaganda, 103
prosperity, 4, 82, 139
prostitutes, 98, 132–3